The Way, The Truth & The Life Series

The Truth

Teacher's Book

Second Edition

By Sr Marcellina Cooney CP

Editorial Team

Doug Doherty, Angela Edwards, Angela Grady, Stephen Horsman,

James Jukes, Liz McCaul, Paul Moloney, Rachel Smith and Mary White

Publisher

Teachers' Enterprise in Religious Education Co. Ltd

Second and extensively revised edition: April 2010

A joint enterprise by
Teachers' Enterprise in Religious Education Co. Ltd and Sr Marcellina Cooney CP

Nihil Obstat: Fr Anton Cowan – Censor

Imprimatur: The Most Reverend Vincent Nichols PhL, MA, Med, STL
                          Archbishop of Westminster
                          18 March 2010 - Feast of St Cyril of Jerusalem

Nihil Obstat and *Imprimatur* are declarations that the books are free from doctrinal or moral error. It is not implied that those who have granted the *Nihil Obstat* and the *Imprimatur* agree with the contents, opinions or statements expressed.

Theological Advisor: Fr Herbert Alphonso SJ

Curriculum Advisor: Joe Fitzpatrick

Picture Research: Sr Marcellina Cooney & Ian Curtis

ISBN 978-0-9566629-1-0

Published by
Teachers' Enterprise in Religious Education Co. Ltd
40 Duncan Terrace
Islington
London N1 8A

Printed in the UK by The Magazine Printing Company plc

Introduction

Welcome to the second edition of 'The Truth' Teacher's Book which accompanies the Student's Book and DVD ROM. These form part of the series 'The Way, the Truth & the Life' which has now been published for 3 – 14 year olds.

This programme is based on the Catechism of the Catholic Church and the Religious Education Curriculum Directory for Catholic Schools published by the Bishops' Conference. The great strength of this series is its theological content linked in an imaginative way to the world of young people today.

'The Truth' builds on 'The Way' and ensures continuity and progression. In this second edition, there is an in-depth study of 'Creation'; what it means to be made in the image and likeness of God and the importance of stewardship with reference to current ecological issues. The module, 'Covenant' enables you to give students an overview of Salvation History and leads into the fulfilment of the new covenant in Jesus through the 'Mystery of the Eucharist' and the 'Paschal Mystery'. The 'Mission of the Church' highlights many of the opportunities there are for helping others. This leads to the 'Church in Britain' which helps us to reflect on the past and consider the privileges and freedom we enjoy today, thanks to the faith and commitment of missionaries and martyrs.

On the DVD ROM, you will find support in the variety of additional resources. Together with the Teacher's and Student's Books, the DVD ROM has been produced by the Teachers' Enterprise in Religious Education Co. Ltd, that is, by teachers from different parts of the country working in a collaborative manner and pooling their expertise.

I thank Fr. Herbert Alphonso SJ warmly for all the work he has put into the theological notes, the study sessions in Rome and for the great encouragement he continually gives to the teachers involved in the Enterprise.

I trust that all who use this Teacher's Book, Student's Book, DVD ROM and the supporting website www.tere.org will be helped in a clear and direct way in the important task of enabling students to learn about the Catholic faith and to respond to its invitation with growing faith and generosity.

✠ Vincent Nichols

✠ Vincent Nichols
Archbishop of Westminster

Contents

1. Creation

2. The Covenant

3. Mystery of the Eucharist

4. The Paschal Mystery

5. The Mission of the Church

6. The Church in Britain

Overview of Key Stage 3 Syllabus

	Autumn 1	Autumn 2	Spring 1	Spring 2	Summer 1	Summer 2
THE WAY Year 7	Revelation & Faith	God's Promises Fulfilled	The Saviour	The Church	The Sacraments	Christianity & Other Faiths
THE TRUTH Year 8	Creation	Covenant	Mystery of the Eucharist	Paschal Mystery	Mission of the Church	The Church in Britain
THE LIFE Year 9	Spiritual Quest	Dialogue with Other Faiths	The Gospels	Life in the Spirit	God's Call	Conscience

Notes For Users

The series *The Way, the Truth & the Life* has been published for 3 – 14 year olds. The text book for Year 8 was the first to be published in 2001. This new edition of *The Truth* replaces it.

The contents of this **Teacher's** Book, **Student's** Book and DVD ROM are based on the Catechism of the Catholic Church and the Religious Education Curriculum Directory for Catholic Schools, Bishops' Conference of England & Wales, 1996.

The **DVD ROM** to support *The Truth* offers an extensive variety of resources: Power Point Presentations; audio recordings; flipcharts for Smart and Promethean interactive whiteboards; together with creative worksheets to stimulate and motivate all abilities. There are two videos on Taizé, one lasting fifteen and the other nine minutes. You may need to download DIVX software from the Internet for best quality viewing.

There is a Power Point presentation on 'Assessment for Learning' for training teachers and a wide range of assessment tasks mapped to the Levels of Attainment in Religious Education in Catholic Schools and Colleges, Bishops' Conference publication 2007.

This **DVD ROM** is published by the Teachers' Enterprise in Religious Education Co. Ltd; details can be found on the supporting website www.tere.org

KEY to symbols and abbreviations in this Teacher's Book:

 WS (with a number) = Worksheet on the DVD ROM

 PPP = Power Point Presentation on the DVD ROM

 Flipcharts for Smart and Promethean interactive whiteboards on the DVD ROM

 Audio recording on the DVD ROM

 Reflective activity or prayer

 Assessment Tasks

CCC = Catechism of the Catholic Church

RECD = Religious Education Curriculum Directory, Bishops' Conference of England and Wales

Tips For Teaching & Learning

- As students enter the classroom have something for them to do right away.
- Write down the key learning objective (KLO).
- Ask probing questions to find out what they already know about the KLO. Expect more than superficial answers.
- Remember it helps to start with a question rather than a statement.
- Recap on the previous lesson by asking a series of probing questions.
- Students record new words and their meaning.
- Use new words to make sentences to show the meaning.
- Play 'Lucky dip': a student picks a key word out of a box, then has to explain that word and what they know about it.
- Or 'Just a minute': a student selects a word from the board and talks about it for a minute.
- Or 'Guess my word': a student picks a word out of a box and talks about it without saying the word. The rest of the group guess the word as quickly as possible.
- Quick quiz: students stand behind their chairs for a quick quiz on key words and only sit down when they have given the correct answer.

Students need to feel they are being challenged and kept on the alert.

Purpose & Relevance:

The main part of the lesson is introduced by the teacher telling the students what they are going to learn, rather than what they are going to do. Lessons have focus. Students need to perceive a purpose and relevance in what they are doing. It will help if they have a copy of the Key Learning Objectives in their exercise books and are able to tick them off as soon as they have been achieved.

Another feature is the active teaching. For example, the teacher will demonstrate but at the same time involve students by constantly asking probing questions. The brain functions best when it is engaged in a constant variety of activities rather than passively absorbing information.

Frequently ask students to stop, think, suggest and explain. They might have a moment to talk to a partner, bounce ideas off each other and come up with suggestions. The teacher facilitates the process rather than directs the entire sequence.

A key feature is asking students to explain their thinking or working out. Invite students to come to the front of the class to do so. It is helpful to highlight good ways of working and show how good learners operate. Encourage them to take responsibility for their own learning.

Importance of Reflection:

Reflection is crucial to the learning process. It helps students to see the relevance of what they are learning for their own lives or the lives of others. Encourage them to make links with their daily lives in school, at home or the area in which they live.

Plenaries:

The lesson closes with a plenary session in which the teacher draws out the key points. Students do most of the work. They are encouraged to explain what they've learned and how it can be used. Regular homework helps individuals to consolidate what they have learned in the lesson or to prepare for the next one.

The final plenary is an opportunity to round off, summarise the lesson and to underline what has been accomplished. It helps students to focus on the most important rather the most recent points, what they have learned and the progress they have made. It should aim to refocus students on the objectives that have featured in the lesson. It is also a time to look back and look forward, and to relate work in the lesson to real life situations.

Plenaries are also useful part way through a lesson: a moment to pause when the teacher draws the class together, checks understanding and directs the class to the next phase of work.

Plenaries will vary in length, two minutes on one day, twenty minutes on another, depending on the style and format of what the teacher has planned. To provide the necessary variety, they can be used to:
- draw together what has been learned, to highlight the most important rather than the most recent points, to summarise key facts, ideas and vocabulary, and stress what needs to be remembered;
- question students and rectify any remaining misunderstandings;
- make links to other work and what the class will go on to do next;
- highlight the progress students have made and remind them about their personal targets;
- set homework to extend or consolidate class work and prepare for future lessons.

In drawing the lesson together, the vital part is helping students to think about what they may have learned by getting them to summarise the ideas in the lesson.

Ultimately learning should be an adventure with a sense of enjoyment. If lessons have meaning and purpose for the lives of the students they will want to be involved.

Teachers should set high expectations for themselves, live up to them and then encourage the students to do the same.

Assessment for Learning:

In preparation for teaching each module, it is best to have chosen an assessment task from the folder 'Assessment Tasks & Levels' in advance. This should not be an 'end of module test' but used as a classroom activity that will be marked in depth and awarded a 'level of attainment'.

DVD ROM: PPP 'Assessment for Learning'

Contents of DVD ROM

Introduction – Archbishop Vincent Nichols

Notes for users

Overview of Key Stage 3 Syllabus

Syllabus 'The Truth'

Theology of the Bible

Ways to Differentiate

Ways to teach Key Words

PPP Assessment for Learning

8.1 Creation
Power Point Presentation (PPP)

1. Spring
2. Summer
3. Autumn
4. Winter
5. Ryan's Well
6. Sr. Dorothy Stang
7. Globalisation
8. Vatican Observatory
9. Catechism of the Catholic Church

Worksheets

WS 1 Theological/Scientific Truths
WS 2 The Creation
WS 3 Whose fault was it? (for less able students)
WS 4 De-creator responds
WS 5 Ryan's Well
WS 6 Stewards of the Earth
WS 7 Canticle of St. Francis

Other Resources

Key Words
How to use the Catechism
Creation Stories
Reforming the Calendar – Vatican Observatory

Flipcharts For Promethean & Smart

Psalm 139
Poem "Earth's crammed with Heaven"
Made in the image of God
Human ecology
Original Sin
Ecology
Notes on Flipcharts

Audio Recordings

Close your Eyes Reflection
Psalm 139
Birds of the Air & Two Sparrows
Creation of man & woman, the Fall

Assessment

Twelve Assessment Tasks and Levels

8.2 The Covenant
Power Points

1. Creation & Noah
2. Abraham
3. Joseph
4. Moses Parts 1 & 2
5. The Plagues
6. David
7. Solomon & Exile
8. Prophets
9. Covenants
10. The Annunciation
11. Advent
12. The Nativity

Worksheets

WS 1 The Seder at our house
WS 2 Israelites: Faith, Challenge, Blessing
WS 3 Multiple choice quiz
WS 4 Ten Commandments – guided thinking
WS 5 Ten Commandments Today
WS 6 Moses: Faith, Challenge, Blessing
WS 7 Covenant Rules
WS 8 Crossword
WS 9 Covenants – guided thinking
WS 10 Poem: Yet if His Majesty our Sovereign Lord
WS 11 Visit of the Magi

Other Resources

Key Words
Joseph's Happiness Chart
Seder Night at our house
Advent Service

Flipcharts For Promethean & Smart

Difference between Covenant & Contract
Commandments
Notes on Flipcharts

Audio Recordings
The Ten Commandments
Jeremiah - Covenant

Assessment
Ten Assessment Tasks and Levels

8.3 Mystery Of The Eucharist
Power Points
1. Sign of the Cross
2. 'I am the bread of life' Pope Benedict XVI
3. Why go to Mass? Pope Benedict XVI
4. The Eucharist Pope Benedict XVI
5. The Last Supper
6. The Lamb of God
7. Maximilian Kolbe
8. Vestments & Vessels

Worksheets
WS 1   A New Commandment – Guided thinking
WS 2   Why go to Mass?
WS 3   Signs & symbols at Mass
WS 4   Overview of the Mass
WS 5   Order of the Mass
WS 6   Five ways to participate at Mass

Other Resources
Key Words
Love One Another – Reflection
Psalm 23
Reflection on Psalm 23

Flipcharts For Promethean & Smart
The New Covenant
Reasons for going to Mass
Signs & Symbols
The Penitential Rite
The Liturgy of the Word
The Offertory
Abraham in the Eucharistic Prayer
The Consecration
Notes on Flipcharts

Audio Recordings
A New Commandment

Assessment
Eleven Assessment Tasks & Levels

8.4 The Paschal Mystery
Power Points
1. Passion Sunday in Church
2. Holy Thursday Mass
3. Altar of Repose on Holy Thursday
4. Judas
5. Trial before the Sanhedrin
6. Jesus before Pilate
7. Centurion's Monologue
8. Good Friday in Church
9. Easter Vigil in Church

Worksheets
WS 1   Donkey Owner (for less able students)
WS 2   Holy Week record of events
WS 3   Gethsemane
WS 4   Jesus before the Sanhedrin
WS 5   Witnesses
WS 6   Man to Man: Nicodemus & Pilate
WS 7   Man to Man: Nicodemus & Pilate (Ext.)
WS 8   Peter looks back
WS 9   Emperor to Pilate
WS 10 Pilate points the finger
WS 11 Why is the suffering and death of Jesus
       important to Christians?

Other Resources
Key Words
Centurion's Monologue script
The Passion (for three voices)
The Cross in my pocket
Holy Week: What Jesus did & how we remember it now

Flipcharts For Promethean & Smart
Judas
Peter's character
Peter & Judas under pressure
Mary of Magdala
Notes on Flipcharts

Audio Recordings
Donkey Owner
Centurion's Monologue
Garden of Gethsemane
The Way of Sorrows
Easter Sunday

Assessment
Eleven Assessment Tasks & Levels

8.5 The Mission Of The Church
Power Points
1. St. Thérèse in Britain
2. A Missionary Sister in the Philippines
3. The Passage
4. The Columban Sisters in Peru
5. St. Alberto Hurtado SJ
6. Taizé
7. Video of Taizé
   Plenaries to recap:
8. Church as People of God
9. Church as Body of Christ
10. Church as Community

Worksheets
WS 1 Mission of St. Thérèse of Lisieux
WS 2 The Passage
WS 3 Activity using hamburger
WS 4 Dorothy Day
WS 5 Pauline Jaricot
WS 6 Bl. Teresa of Calcutta
WS 7 The Power of Forgiveness

Other Resources
Key Words
Fr. William in L'Arche (full text)
Poster on Taizé

Flipcharts For Promethean & Smart
Challenges to Christianity
Church as Body of Christ
Church as Community
Living the Mission
St. Alberto Hurtado SJ
L'Arche
Notes on Flipcharts

Audio Recordings
Dorothy Day
Mother Teresa

Assessment
Ten Assessment Tasks & Levels

8.6 Christianity In Britain
Power Points
1. St. David
2. Angels not Angles
3. Conscience
4. Priests' Hiding Holes
5. Some English Martyrs
6. St. John Fisher

Worksheets
WS 1 Disciples' Journey of Faith
WS 2 Faith Journey (3 pages for pair work)
WS 3 St. Patrick
WS 4 St. Columba
WS 5 Monastic life in the Middle Ages
WS 6 Dissolution of the Monasteries
WS 7 What is special about the Catholic Church?

Other Resources
Key Words
St. Hilda
St. Aidan
St. David
St. Brigid
Trial of Thomas More from 'A Man for All Seasons' (Act III Condensed)
Letter from Margaret Clitherow

Flipcharts For Promethean & Smart
Alban and the Priest
Notes on Flipcharts

Audio Recordings
St. Alban
'A Man for all Seasons' (extract)
St. Margaret Clitherow
Some changes in the Catholic Church since Vatican II
Pope John Paul II

Assessment
Fourteen Assessment Tasks & Levels

Note: Note: This DVD ROM has been developed for teachers, by teachers working on a voluntary basis. It is **illegal to copy** this disc for another school and should you do so you will not only be breaking the law but you will also be depriving your colleagues of income necessary to develop further resources for you.

8.1 Creation

Religious Education Curriculum Directory

"Creation is the first and universal revelation of God's love. Each human person is unique and made in God's image and likeness". (p. 14)

Catechism of the Catholic Church

"Nothing exists that does not owe its existence to God the Creator. The world began when God's word drew it out of nothingness; all existent beings, all of nature, and all human history are rooted in this primordial event, the very genesis by which the world was constituted and time begun." (CCC 338, also 364-366)

Attainment Target 1: Learning *about* the Catholic faith.
Attainment Target 2: Learning *from* the Catholic faith.

Key Learning Objectives:

- Know that God created and sustains the world.
  o Reflect on some of the wonders of Creation.

- Understand the theological truths in the accounts of Creation in Genesis.
  o Reflect on their importance for us.

- Know that we are made in the image and likeness of God.
  o Reflect on what this means for us.

- Understand the account of the Fall in Genesis.
  o Reflect on the consequences of this for us.

- Understand God's call to stewardship.
  o Reflect on our response to it.

- Know about people whose lives were deeply influenced by God's Creation.
  o Think about how we can learn from them to live simply.

Theological Notes

8.1 Creation

Christian tradition from the earliest times has attributed to God the Father the work of creation – the creation of the whole universe. As we profess in the Apostles' Creed: "I believe in God the Father Almighty, Creator of heaven and earth", or in the Nicene Creed: We believe in one God, the Father, the Almighty, maker of heaven and earth, of all that is visible and invisible". So **God the Father** is acknowledged as **the Creator and Origin of all things**, visible and invisible, in the entire cosmos.

One immediate consequence of this fundamental Christian belief for the whole range of our practical Christian living is that we should give God a real and serious chance to be God in our lives. We should try to do this, not just globally as it were in one all-encompassing act performed once and for all, but in the several daily details of our everyday living. As the celebrated mystic of the 14th century, Meister Eckhart, admirably couched this practical challenge: 'Let go, let God'.

Made in the image and likeness of God (Gen. 1:26-27)

The Hebrew verb 'barά' (to create) which is used in Genesis 1:1 (In the beginning God **created** heaven and earth) is used again *three times* in Genesis 1:27 (God created man in his own image, in the image of God he created him, male and female he created them'). This verb is used to indicate an action especially and exclusively divine. The creation of the human person ('man') marks the *culminating peak* of this account of creation.

Note that verse 27 is preceded by a kind of consultation (among the three Divine Persons), for it says: "Let *us* make the human person ('man') after our own image and likeness (verse 26). This implies: the human person's place and role is 'highlighted' as God's 'lieutenant' with the triple use of the verb 'to create' – that is, his/her divine image and likeness makes him/her have 'dominion' over the rest of creation expressed in responsibility to be exercised as the 'representative' of God; in other words, a responsibility and respect in the exercise of true 'freedom', which is a sharing in God's 'freedom'. The differentiation in complementary 'sexuality' (male-female) is in the image and likeness of the 'communion' among the three Divine Persons (Let *us* make 'man' after our image and likeness: Gen. 1:26). God's evaluation of his work of creation "… very good"! (Gen 1:31).

Freedom

In what sense are we free to make our own decisions?

Many Christians, when faced with decision-making adopt a stance which may be formulated as follows: 'I am free to make my decision. Certainly, I shall think and reflect, weigh up the reasons for and against, perhaps seek counsel or advice, and then I am free to make my decision'. In all this, one fundamental factor seems to be overlooked, if not neglected and completely forgotten. Every human freedom is a created freedom; as such, it is under God – God the Creator and Origin of all things. If every human freedom is under God, so too – and even more so – is every Christian freedom; this means that no decision can genuinely be taken by anyone without first letting God be God in the process of that particular decision-making, that is, without first seeking what God wants of that person, for God has a plan, a design, His will for that person and his/her life. In other words, LETTING GO – LETTING GOD is a first and essential step in genuine decision-making. Only once a person has become aware of God's plan or will for him/her, may that person then actively receive it in his/her life and make it his/her own. This is when a true and authentic decision is taken.

Original Sin

Essential Truth of Catholic Faith

The Catholic doctrine on **'original sin'** is, as it were, the 'counterpart or 'correlative' part of the Good News that Jesus Christ is the Saviour of all men and women, that all are in need of salvation and that this salvation is offered to all human beings thanks to Jesus Christ (see Rom. 5:12-21). We firmly believe that any weakening in our acceptance of what divine revelation teaches us on 'original sin' would involve a corresponding undermining of the salvific and redemptive mystery of Jesus Christ.

God created man and woman out of love. He created them in a state of holiness or righteousness, which means, in a relationship of friendship with Him: and God who created them in His image and likeness gave them the gift of 'freedom' or liberty, so that they could *freely* choose to be who they really were, namely 'creatures' of God their 'Creator'. In other words, God wanted them, because He loved them, to freely be and live in friendship with Him.

This was God's loving plan not only for Adam and Eve but, inasmuch as they were the 'first parents' of all humankind, also for all men and women after them – for all members of the human race. Such a 'unity' of the entire human race – or 'solidarity' of all human beings – is part of God's loving plan for all of humankind.

However, from the very dawn of history, man and woman were tempted by the Evil One. They mis-used their God-given gift of 'freedom' to turn against their Creator: they sought to find their self-fulfilment apart from God and from His plan for their life of friendship and happiness with Him.

By this turning against God, Adam and Eve lost their original state of righteousness or relationship of friendship with God. God had intended His original plan of friendship with Him for all human beings in and through their 'first parents' Adam and Eve – in virtue of what we have called above the 'unity' or 'solidarity' of the entire human race, therefore, by their turning against God, Adam and Eve lost that original state of friendship with God for all human beings coming after them. In this sense, Adam and Eve passed on to their descendants in the human race their human nature wounded by their 'first sin' and therefore deprived them of the original state of righteousness or friendship with God. **This deprivation of the original state of friendship with God is called *original sin*.**

We have just said that original sin was passed on to all members of the human race – to all, except to Our Lady, the Blessed Virgin Mary who, by a special privilege in virtue of the victory that Jesus Christ to be born of her would win through His death and resurrection over the powers of sin and death, was preserved from this deprivation or 'taint' of *original sin*. This privilege, which we call Our Lady's 'Immaculate Conception', was granted her by God in view of her very specially close and intimate association with her Son, Jesus Christ, in his entire mystery of redeeming us as our Saviour.

The deprivation called *'original sin'* implies that our human nature is wounded weakened, submitted to a 'darkening of the mind' or 'ignorance'. Also, it is subject to suffering, to the powers and forces of 'death', to an innate inclination or tendency towards 'sin' – this tendency is termed 'concupiscence'.

While all such 'woundedness' and weakening of our human nature does not by itself amount to culpable fault or sin, we must never forget that the victory won by Jesus Christ through his paschal mystery of passion, death and resurrection has obtained for us benefits and gifts far superior to those of which we were deprived through the original sin of our 'first parents'. For "where sin abounded, grace has abounded all the more" (Rom 5:20). We Christians see the world as created and sustained in existence by the love of God, its Creator; this world, through man and woman, fell into the bondage of sin, but God's redeeming love has freed it from this slavery and transformed it anew in and through the crucifixion, death and resurrection of Jesus Christ His Son, who, in this way, broke the stranglehold of the Evil One over it.

Herbert Alphonso SJ

Notes on Genesis 1-11:
There are two traditions behind chapters 1-11, the Priestly (P) and the Yahwist (J).

In Genesis 1, the Priestly creation account is a mature statement of faith about God's relationship with the world and with the creatures in it. This story shows that God's purpose is written into creation – a purpose of order, beauty and obedience as opposed to chaos.

In Genesis 2, the Yahwist creation story is a dramatic account of creation and fall. The characters are representative. Both accounts of creation use the language and imagery of the ancient Mesopotamian myths, but the accounts are adapted to convey the faith of Israel and refute the message of the pagan myths. For example, it seems clear that the author(s) of the Priestly account of creation was aware of the Babylonian epic, the Enuma Elish, or something similar to it. However, the theological content of Genesis chapter 1 is different. In Genesis 1, there is one God not many as in Enuma Elish. Human beings are made in the image of God and have responsibility over creation. In Genesis 2, the Yahwist author uses elements from the pagan myths but the theology is different: God begins with the creation of human beings and they are given a beautiful world to cultivate. Sin and evil come, not from God but from human choice.

Additional Suggestions and Resources

> ## Know that God created and sustains the world.
> ## Reflect on some of the wonders of Creation.

Starting Point:

Transform your classroom before students arrive. Make sure it reflects some of the beauty of creation: posters and some colourful plants. Try to awaken in students a deeper appreciation of the beauty of all living things: trees, plants, flowers, insects, animals, birds, etc.

 Audio Recording: 'Close your eyes'. If possible darken the room to create a reflective atmosphere.

 PPPs: The four Power Point presentations: autumn, winter, spring, summer could be used as a silent meditation at the start of lessons or just for the first lesson.

Encourage students to take photos of nature to create a display for the classroom.

 Flipcharts: Psalm 139.

 Audio Recording: Psalm 139.

 Flipcharts: Poem 'Earth's crammed with Heaven'.

 Assessment Folder: 'God does not create to forget but *creates and sustains*'. *Discuss.*

To conclude: Let us take time to think of the most important points of this study for us personally *(allow time)*. What could you plan to do to ensure you do not take for granted God's gift of creation and his personal gifts to you?

> ## Understand the theological truths in the accounts of Creation in Genesis.
> ## Reflect on their importance for us.

Note: The early chapters of Genesis are neither science nor history; their purpose is a religious one. They are, first of all, a theological statement. Be aware that this section may be quite challenging for some students.

Starting Point:

Give examples to explain the difference between a scientific truth and a theological truth.

 WS 1: Scientific and theological truths on DVD ROM.

 Audio Recording: 'The Creation' radio discussion.

Beliefs about Creation: Students's book page 8 gives a brief outline of the different theories.

WS 2: 'The Creation' is a more detailed explanation of the different theories of Creation for a role-play.

 PPP: The Vatican Observatory.

 Assessment Folder - three tasks:

Choose a tree, plant, flower or leaf. Describe in a scientific way and in a theological way how it came into existence.

a) Explain how people who believe in God understand the account of Creation.
b) Explain how some scientists understand the story.

"It is not possible to be a scientist and believe in God'. Discuss.

To conclude: Let us remind ourselves of what we have learned. What are the most important facts to remember?

> ### Know that we are made in the image and likeness of God.
> ### Reflect on what this means for us.

Note: This may be the most difficult section in this module so there is a need to take it slowly to make sure students understand and have grasped the most important points.

Starting point:

In what ways are we different from animals? Does anyone know why?

Poem: This is You, page 9, use as a reflection. Help students to reflect on their wonderful God-given qualities and to thank God for them.

Flipcharts: Made in the image of God. The quotations from the Catechism of the Catholic Church on pages 10-11 are difficult but the flipcharts are intended to simplify them for the less able students.

 Audio Recordings: 'Birds of the air' (Mt. 6:25-34); 'Two Sparrows' (Mt. 10:29-31).

Reflection: A Life that Matters: This reflection is very challenging so it is important to explain to students that we must earnestly pray for God's grace to be able to forgive; sometimes it is very difficult.

 Flipcharts: Human Ecology.

 Assessment Folder: Assessment sheet on the dignity of the human body.

Assessment task: 'We are God's work of art...'

To conclude: Invite students to share what they consider to be the most important points they have learned. Ask them to think of a way of remembering them.

> ## Understand the account of the Fall in Genesis.
> ## Reflect on the consequences of this for us.

Note: Read notes on original sin on page 14.
It will be helpful if you have collected some newspaper headlines to use as illustrations of various types of suffering in our world.

Starting Point:
The presence of evil and suffering in our world is very difficult and there are no easy answers. Nevertheless, it is important to give students the opportunity to raise questions.

 Audio Recording: Genesis 2:18-24 & 3:1-24. Creation of man and woman and the Fall.

 WS 3: Whose fault was it? (For less able students)

 Flipcharts: Original Sin.

Note: Evidence that Mary was without sin: In the RSV translation of the Bible Lk. 1:28 the angel Gabriel greets Mary as "Hail, full of grace". In the traditional prayer of the Church "Hail Mary, full of grace, the Lord is with thee." At Lourdes, Mary told St. Bernadette Soubirous, "I am the Immaculate Conception".

Assessment Folder: The three activities on page 16 have levels of attainment.

> **Understand God's call to stewardship.**
> **Reflect on our response to it.**

Starting Point:

Reflection: Invite students to sit comfortably and try to open their hearts to those who are hungry.
When was the last time you were hungry?
How did it feel?
Think of all those who are hungry right now in the world.
Let us pray for those who are about to die of hunger.
Lord, we do not have in our hands the solutions for the problems of the world. But we have our own hands! Help us now to keep our minds and hearts open to see what we can do with our hands.

 PPP: Globalisation.

 Flipcharts: Ecology.

 WS 4: Creator - De-creator.

 WS 5: Ryan's Story. Website www.ryanswell.ca

 WS 6: Stewards of the Earth, Research Task. (TB & DVD ROM)

 Assessment Folder:
'It's man's greed not man's need that has created the imbalance in the universe'. Discuss.
There is an additional task on developing and utilising the earth's resources.

Prayer:
Lord God,
Give us courage when things go wrong: strengthen us with faith in you, with hope in your promises and with love of your will.

Guide our thoughts, our words, our actions, so that what we do today may be pleasing to you.
Amen

> **Know about people whose lives were deeply influenced by God's Creation.**
> **Reflect on how we can learn from them to live simply.**

Note: Students move quickly from one subject to another so for religious education it is important to create a conducive atmosphere, something that makes RE special, that will help them to open their minds and hearts to the sacred.

Starting Point:

Create a reflective atmosphere by showing one of the **Power Point** presentations on autumn, winter, spring or summer. You may wish to have some soft music in the background. You may wish them to share what the lessons on 'Creation' have meant to them. What are they more aware of now?

 WS 7: Canticle of St. Francis. (for activity on page 20 SB in TB and DVD ROM)

Student's Book page 21: invite students to study the illustration of Blessed Kateri Tekakwitha to see if they can find the dove and the crucifix in it. Then read the text to find out why the illustrator chose to include them.

 PPP: Sr. Dorothy Stang.

<u>www.tere.org</u> Go to 'Secondary' and click on KS3 Support Material to find 'St. Francis'.

 Assessment Tasks: Sr. Dorothy Stang.

Live Simply

Compassionate and loving God,
you created the world for all of us to share,
a world of beauty and plenty.
create in us a desire to live simply,
so that our lives may reflect your generosity.

Creator God,
You gave us responsibility for the earth,
a world of riches and delight.
Create in us a desire to live sustainably,
so that those who follow after us
may enjoy the fruits of your creation.
Amen
© CAFOD

Ryan's Story

Ryan Hreljac is a student at St. Michael's Catholic School in Canada. In January 1998, when Ryan was six years old and in Year 1, his teacher told the class about people in Africa who were dying because they had no clean water - just $70 (£30) would be enough to sink a well and save their lives. Ryan asked his mum and dad for $70. They explained that this was a lot of money, they just could not give it to him, but they would give him the chance to do extra jobs to earn it.

After four months of cleaning the house, washing dishes and windows, Ryan had raised the money, but sadly when he contacted 'Watercan' the Canadian Charity, he was told that building a well costs $2,000 (£857). Ryan did not give up: he took on more jobs and started giving talks and had fundraising activities. His first talk at a Rotary Club raised several hundred dollars. His story soon appeared in the local newspaper and 'Watercan' received hundreds of dollars in donations. Ryan was able to pay for his first well in autumn 1998.

Since then, schools in Canada and the United States have held fundraising events and Ryan's Well Foundation has raised over $800,000 (£343,000) which has paid for more than seventy wells in Uganda, Ethiopia, Kenya, Malawi, Zimbabwe, Nigeria and Tanzania. An estimated 150,000 people now have clean water as a result.

When Ryan was nine years old, he went with his parents to see his first well. Five thousand men, women and children lined the dry dusty road that led to the well and chanted his name. Jimmy, his pen pal, was among them. Before they got the well, Jimmy had to rise in the middle of the night every night to walk eight kilometres to get water. "I had to go back and back again to fill the pot at home. Then I went to school. The water was not clean, it looked like chocolate", he said.

Ryan's parents discovered that Jimmy was an orphan, so they wanted to adopt him but then they heard the horrifying news: Jimmy had been kidnapped with four of his cousins by guerrillas who wanted to turn them into child soldiers. The family could do nothing but wait and worry. A few days later they were told that Jimmy had escaped; he had seen two of his cousins shot dead so he chewed through the ropes that bound him and ran off into the bush.

In May 2003, Jimmy arrived in Canada and was granted refugee status. Now, he goes to school with Ryan. His favourite subjects are Religion and English – and he's the school's top male runner.

Activity

1. What age do you think Ryan was when he gave his first talk to business men at the Rotary Club?

2. In what ways do you think Ryan's story might inspire other young people to help those in great need?

3. Use the Internet to find out what Ryan is now doing to help others and write an UPDATE on Ryan's Well - www.ryanswell.ca

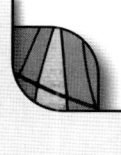

Canticle of St. Francis

"Praise to You, my Lord, for all your creatures,
Above all Brother Sun,
Who brings us the day and lends us his light.
Lovely is he, radiant with great splendour,
And speaks to us of You,
Most High!

Praise to You, my Lord, for Sister Moon and all the stars,
Which You have set in the heavens,
Clear, precious and fair.

Praise to You, my Lord, for Brother Wind,
For air and cloud, for calm and all weather,
By which You support life in all your creatures.

Praise to You, my Lord, for Sister Water,
Who is so useful and humble,
Precious and pure.

Praise to You, my Lord, for Brother Fire,
By whom You light the night;
He is lovely and kind, mighty and strong.

Praise to You, my Lord, for our sister, Mother Earth,
Who comforts and looks after us,
And brings forth fruits, right-coloured flowers and herbs.

Praise and bless my Lord,
Thank Him and serve Him,
With all humility."

 **Activity**

Imagine you are St. Francis. Prepare a 60 second sermon for the people and the birds who flock to hear you preach!
Use words which will:
- awaken people to the beauty of creation;
- encourage them to lavish care on and protect the environment;
- inspire them to give thanks to God.

Scientific and Theological Truths

1. Look at the list below. Decide which is a Scientific Truth and which is a Theological Truth.
   Copy the letter into your exercise book and put 'S' or 'T' beside it to indicate your choice, for example: a) T
   Now write two of your own scientific and two theological truths into your exercise book.

   a) God created the universe.
   b) Coal is the result of decaying trees millions of years old.
   c) When water is frozen it becomes ice.
   d) God loves me.
   e) Light travels at 186,000 miles per second.
   f) Life is a gift from God.
   g) Humans are responsible for looking after the earth.
   h) Life on earth began 2.5 billion years ago.

2. Study the following statements. Select and copy into your exercise book the statements that are true and omit the ones that are not true.

The Bible tells us:
   a) When Creation took place, there was nothing, the next moment everything was there.
   b) In its original form, everything in creation was good.
   c) Before Creation, God existed.
   d) Humans can do whatever they like to the world and everything in it.
   e) There is a balance in Nature that can be disrupted.
   f) Mankind was the final stage in creation, the fulfilment of God's plan.

Science says:
   g) The Universe evolved over billions of years.
   h) There are many things about the earth that we still cannot explain.
   i) God created the heavens and the earth.
   j) Life on earth might have started in the seas, followed by amphibians, reptiles, birds and mammals.
   k) By failing to care for the environment, the balance of Nature can be easily disrupted.
   l) The Universe started with the 'big bang'.

8.2 The Covenant

Religious Education Curriculum Directory

"The action of God in the unfolding history of the covenant relationship and the variety of human response is revealed in the Scriptures of the Old and New Testament." (p. 14)

Catechism of the Catholic Church

"After the patriarchs, God formed Israel as his people by freeing them from slavery in Egypt. He established with them the covenant of Mount Sinai and, through Moses, gave them his law so that they would recognise him and serve him as the one living and true God, the provident Father and just judge, and so they would look for the promised Saviour." (CCC 62)

"Through the prophets, God forms his people in the hope of salvation, in the expectation of a new and everlasting Covenant intended for all, to be written on their hearts." (CCC 64)

Attainment Target 1: Learning *about* the Catholic faith.
Attainment Target 2: Learning *from* the Catholic faith.

Key Learning Objectives:

- Understand the meaning of covenant.
  - o Reflect on some of the covenants God has made.

- Know that God chose Moses to lead His people towards the Promised Land.
  - o Reflect on God's choice of leader.

- Know how the Jews celebrate the Passover today.
  - o Reflect on why the Jews celebrate the Passover.

- Know about the Exodus.
  - o Think about the message it has for us today.

- Know about God's covenant with His Chosen People.
  - o Reflect on what we can learn from it.

- Know that God sent the prophets to remind the people of His covenant and unfailing love for them.
  - o Reflect on the message of the prophets for us today.

- Understand that Jesus has come and has made a New Covenant with us.
  - o Prepare to celebrate the birth of Jesus.

Theological Notes

The Call of Moses

Moses was tending the flock of sheep of his father-in-law Jethro. As he was leading the sheep into the wilderness, he came to the mountain of God, Horeb. There God appeared to him in the burning bush. What Moses saw was the bush aflame; but the bush, he noticed, was not being consumed by the flames. So Moses became curious; it is God's own Word that calls attention to Moses' curiosity. Wanting to understand and grasp this strange phenomenon, he started making a tour of the bush, as it were, to 'master' this phenomenon. Then it was that God spoke out of the bush: "Moses! Moses! Do not come near, stand away from here: this is holy ground. Take off your shoes, your sandals from your feet, for you are standing on holy ground. I am God: the God of your father Abraham, the God of Isaac and the God of Jacob". In other words, God is saying equivalently to Moses: "The only position for you is face-down on the ground, prostrate before me, for I am God – the God of Abraham, of Isaac and of Jacob". And it is not until Moses has moved away from that holy Ground and acknowledged God as God (cf. Ex. 3:6), that he will receive effectively his call and mission from God to be, in God's name, the liberator of God's people from slavery and oppression in Egypt. "I have heard", says God to Moses, "the cry of the people in Egypt, the people enslaved and oppressed. I am sending you to the King of Egypt, to Pharaoh, to ask him to release my people and let them go." We should note Moses' reaction. "Who am I", he says to God, "that I should go to Pharaoh and tell him to let the people go?" "Who am I? I know **you** are God, the God of my fathers Abraham, Isaac and Jacob; I have acknowledged **you** as such. But who am I?" Then it is that God says: "**I** will be with you. Go!" We would do well to pay close attention to these words, which will continually and unfailingly recur in every call and vocation, after God who calls has been acknowledged and worshipped as God: "Do not be afraid, I will be with you. I **am** with you."

The characteristic of God right through the revelation of the Old Testament is **God's faithful love**: He is and remains always, relentlessly so, the God of covenant love, the God who remains unfailingly faithful to His covenant of merciful, forgiving, reconciling and transforming love.

(a) Moses: The first and obvious way we can learn of God's ever faithful love towards the people he chose in love to be his own 'chosen people' is to listen to Moses himself, whom God deputed to lead them from 'slavery' to 'freedom', from being 'no people' to being '**his** chosen people'. In the Book of Deuteronomy, Moses recounts this chosen people's ongoing history of being loved, and pursued in love, by God even when they repeatedly and stubbornly hardened their hearts to reject God and his covenants of love: "You are a people holy to the Lord, your God; the Lord, your God, has chosen you to be a people of his own possession, out of all the peoples that are on the face of the earth. It was not because you were more in number than any other people that the Lord set his love upon you and chose you, for you were the fewest of all people; but it is because the Lord loves you, and is keeping the oath which he swore to your fathers, that the Lord has brought you out with a mighty hand, and redeemed you from the house of bondage … Know therefore that the Lord your God is God, the faithful God who keeps covenant and steadfast love … to a thousand generations" (Deut. 7:6-9).

In forthright language, Moses continues: "Know, therefore, that the Lord is not giving you this land to possess because of your righteousness; for you are a stubborn people. … Furthermore the Lord said to me, 'I have seen this people, and behold it is a stubborn people; let me alone, that I may destroy them and blot out their name from under heaven. … So I lay prostrate before the Lord for these forty days and forty nights, because the Lord had said that he would destroy you. And I prayed to the Lord, 'O Lord God, destroy not your people and your heritage. … Remember your servants Abraham, Isaac and

Jacob; do not regard the stubbornness of this people or their wickedness or their sin. … For they are your people and your heritage, whom you did bring out by your great power and your outstretched arm'" (Deut. 9:6, 13-14, 25-27, 29).

Right up to the conclusion of his mission, Moses would remind the whole assembly and people of Israel of God's relentless faithfulness in keeping and fulfilling his promises even in the face of their stubborn and stiff-necked resistance of infidelity to his covenant of love. So rang out the accents of his song in the ears of the entire assembly of Israel: "Give ear, O heavens, and I will speak … For I will proclaim the name of the Lord, ascribe greatness to our God: a God of faithfulness and without iniquity, just and right is he. They have dealt corruptly with him, they are no longer his children because of their blemish; they are a perverse and wicked generation … For the Lord's portion is his people, Jacob his allotted heritage. He found him in a desert land … he encircled him, he cared for him, he kept him as the apple of his eye. Like an eagle … that flutters over its young, spreading out its wings, catching them, bearing them on its pinions, the Lord alone did lead him" (Deut. 32:1, 3-5, 9-12).

(b) Hosea: After Moses, we shall be helped to deepen our awareness of and faith in, God's faithfulness in fulfilling his promises of love by taking up briefly the Book of the prophet Hosea, who ministers to the northern kingdom of Israel (also called 'Ephraim' after its largest tribe). Outwardly the nation is enjoying a time of prosperity and growth; but inwardly, moral corruption and spiritual adultery permeate the lives of the people. Hosea, instructed by God to marry a woman named Gomer, finds his domestic life to be an accurate and tragic dramatisation of the unfaithfulness of God's people. During his nearly fifty years of prophetic ministry, Hosea repeatedly returns, in God's name, to his threefold message: God abhors the sins of his people; judgement is certain; but God's loyal and faithful love remains and stands equally certain and firm forever. Hosea, whose name means 'Salvation', offers, as God's messenger, the possibility of salvation to this people if only they would turn from idolatry back to God!

The key and central message of Hosea is *the faithful, loyal love of God for his people, Israel:* in fact, the themes of his prophecy's first three chapters echo throughout the rest of the book. The adultery of Gomer (chapter 1) illustrates the sin of Israel (chapters. 4-7); the degradation of Gomer (chapter 2) represents the judgement of Israel (chapters 8-10); and Hosea's redemption of Gomer (chapter 3) pictures the restoration of Israel (chapters 11-14). In his relationship to Gomer, Hosea portrays God's unfailing faithfulness, justice, love and forgiveness towards his people.

It is in Hosea's prophecy that God's love for Israel takes on profoundly delicate, even maternally tender, accents of affection, and this, in the face of repeated rejection: "When Israel was a child, I loved him, and out of Egypt I called my son. The more I called them, the more they went away from me; they kept sacrificing to the Baals and burning incense to idols. Yet it was I who taught Ephraim to walk. I took them up in my arms; but they did not know that I healed them. I led them with cords of compassion, with the bands of love, and I became to them as one who eases the yoke on their jaws and I stooped down to them and fed them" (Hos. 11:1-4).

Do we human beings not tend to judge our God the way we judge one another, with our human norms and standards? God is God – God, who is love, and not one to be judged and appraised by our human standards and worldly norms. Precisely in the very context in which we were listening to Hosea's statement of God's tender love for his recalcitrant people, we hear these remarkable words of God: "My people are bent on turning away from me ... How can I give you up, O Ephraim! How can I hand you over, O Israel! ... My heart recoils within me, my compassion grows warm and tender. I will not execute my fierce anger, I will not again destroy Ephraim; for **I am God and not man**, the Holy One in your midst, and I will not come to destroy" (Hos. 11: 7-9). Such words touch us deeply, for God appears to be well nigh pleading with us: Do not judge me as you judge one another. Remember always, **"I am God, and not man!"**

(c) Isaiah and Jeremiah: Yet, with all this, it is the later great prophets Isaiah and Jeremiah who powerfully communicate to us, in the continuing, chequered history of the chosen people, God's never-failing faithfulness in keeping the Covenant and fulfilling his promises of saving and redeeming them in love.

Isaiah's prophetic ministry, spanning the reigns of four kings of Judah, covers at least forty years. His prophecy has been called 'the entire Bible in miniature'. Indeed, the first thirty-nine chapters are filled with judgement on immoral and idolatrous men and women. Judah has sinned; the surrounding nations have sinned; the whole earth has sinned. God cannot allow that such blatant sin go unpunished for ever. And yet, the final twenty-seven chapters declare an unambiguous, unmistakable message of hope: the Messiah is coming as a Saviour and a conquering King who will, yes, bear a Cross, but precisely so, will wear a triumphant crown of glory. The prophet's name 'Isaiah' *(Yesha 'yahu)* means 'Yahweh is Salvation', so that his very name becomes an excellent summary of the entire Book named after him.

As Isaiah's name suggests, Salvation comes from God, not from men or human resources. God is clearly proclaimed as the supreme Ruler, the sovereign Lord of history and the only Saviour. Because the nation (Judah) does not turn away from its sinful practices, Isaiah announces the ultimate overthrow of Judah. Nevertheless, God remains, and will remain, faithful to his covenant by preserving a godly remnant; God promises salvation and liberation through the coming Messiah. The Saviour will come out of Judah, and accomplish the dual work of redemption and restoration. The Gentiles will come to his light and, with God making all things anew, a universal blessing will finally take place.

The Call of Jeremiah (1:4-10)

God appeared to Jeremiah and said: "Before I formed you in the womb I knew you, and before you were born I consecrated you; I appointed you a prophet to the nations". To this Jeremiah's reaction was: "Ah, Lord God! Behold, I do not know how to speak, for I am only a youth."

The original Hebrew text suggests Jeremiah being taken aback at God's calling **him**, who at the time was a mere teenager, as the unfolding book of Jeremiah makes clear: "Lord, my God, I can only say 'Ah, ah, ah!' I do not know how to speak; I am a mere youth." As with Moses, so once again, the acknowledgement and recognition of God as God and Lord opens the way to effectively receiving the prophetic call and mission. "But the Lord said to me, 'Do not say, I am only a youth for to all to whom I shall send you, you shall go … Be not afraid of them, for I am with you to deliver you'." So God **himself** touches the mouth of Jeremiah and gives him his own word to be proclaimed. "Then the Lord put forth his hand and touched my mouth; and the Lord said to me, 'Behold, I have put my words in your mouth. Go, speak!'"

Whether in the case of Moses, or in that of the prophets Isaiah and Jeremiah, the same pattern is evident. Call, vocation, mission is not received in effect, until God who has the initiative in calling and giving mission is, in fact, recognised, acknowledged and accepted as God, the Almighty Lord.

The **Book of Jeremiah** is the prophecy of a man divinely called in his youth. He comes across as a heartbroken prophet with a heartbreaking message, who labours for more than forty years preaching a message of doom to the stiff-necked people of Judah. Despised and persecuted by his countrymen, Jeremiah bathes his harsh prophecies in tears of compassion. Even though revealing himself as heartbroken, he forthrightly declares, through his sermons and signs, God's unstinting faithfulness in keeping his promises in love, even to the point of establishing a **'new covenant'**.

Jeremiah's name literally means, 'Yahweh throws', perhaps in the sense of laying a foundation; it could effectively be equivalent to: Yahweh establishes, appoints or sends. In Jeremiah, God is shown to be patient and holy: he delays judgement and appeals to his people to repent before it is too late. As the object lesson at the potter's house demonstrates, a ruined vessel can be repaired while still wet (Jer. 18:1-4); but, once dried, a marred vessel is fit only for the garbage heap (Jer. 19:10-11). God's warning is clear: Judah's time for repentance will soon pass. Because the people defy God's words and refuse to repent, the Babylonian captivity and exile are inevitable. While Jeremiah courageously and forthrightly foretells, in God's name, the people's coming catastrophe, he also unambiguously proclaims God's gracious and faithful promise of hope and restoration. There will surely be a good and holy remnant of God's people; indeed, God will establish a **'new covenant'**:

> "Behold the days are coming, says the Lord, when I will make a new covenant with the house of Israel and the house of Judah, not like the covenant which I made with their fathers when I took them by the hand to bring them out of the land of Egypt, my covenant which they broke, though I was their husband, says the Lord. But this is the covenant which I will make with the house of Israel after those days, says the Lord: I will put my law within them, and I will write it upon their hearts, and I will be their God and they shall be my people." (Jer. 31:31-34).

It is the Messiah who will institute this covenant by means of his death and resurrection – his paschal passage.

Preparation for the New Covenant

PART 1

An example from real life may best help to illustrate what we are getting at when we speak of God as the best 'educator', 'teacher', 'trainer' or 'pedagogue' in his guiding his plan of salvation gradually moving to its fulfilment: the movement or passage from the 'Old Covenant' to the 'New Covenant'.

An expert dancer on the stage, or an accomplished pianist performing in a concert hall, evokes in us utter admiration that we spontaneously exclaim, "How freely, how gracefully, he/she dances!" Or, "What an amazing grace and freedom with which this pianist is performing, almost making the piano talk!" Where does such astonishing freedom and grace come from? From hours and hours on end, we know only too well, day-in and day-out, of submitting self to the grinding discipline of the ground rules of dancing or of piano-playing: 'step-one, step-two, step-three' repeatedly practised and exercised over and over again; or the musical scales, 'do-re-mi-fa...' played backwards and forwards, thumped out hundreds and thousands of times repeatedly. But neither the dancer nor the pianist submits self to this grinding, gruelling discipline for its own sake – no! Its whole purpose and end-in-view is to release a 'flexibility' a 'freedom', a 'personal style, art and grace' which singles out and characterises the expert and accomplished artist, the master pianist or the professional dancer. The ground rules of dancing or the laws of piano-playing are now no longer merely within the learned books or volumes which expound them at length, nor even in the scholarly teacher who explains them. They have become in the 'expert dancer' or the 'accomplished pianist' an interior law, an interiorised, assimilated, personalised 'heart and spirit', a personal style, which is what 'inner freedom' is all about. The expert dancer on the stage, whose performance we are contemplating in sheer amazement, is no longer watching his/her step to mark or measure 'step-one, step-two, step-three in succession; if he or she did so, they would ruin the dance!! The performing master pianist is no longer checking where his/her fingers are moving on the piano keys to ensure that he/she is playing the right ones in succession if he or she did so, they would ruin the performance!!

However, there is even more that we need to draw out from the illustration we have chosen. Let us take two highly skilled pianists who are both playing the same masterpiece of Beethoven or Chopin. In our poor human language we often say, "Oh! This master pianist has his own personal 'interpretation' of this particular piece of Beethoven or Chopin". What we are really saying, or meaning to say, is in fact: "The first master pianist is expressing his unrepeatable unique self in playing the very same piece of Beethoven or Chopin. In a word, what comes through in our accomplished master artist's performance is the secret of his/her inner freedom – that is, his/her truest and deepest self, his/her unrepeatable unique self.

It is not difficult to see that what we have just spelt out as the process of genuine Christian 'education' or 'formation' or 'training' or 'pedagogy', in truth the paschal passage from the Old Testament dispensation of 'slavery' to the New Testament dispensation of the 'freedom of the children of God' – to use the forceful vigorous biblical language of St Paul's letter to the Galatians and the Romans (cf. Gal. 4-5; Rom. 8).

> "The spirit you received is not the spirit of slaves bringing fear into your lives again; it is the spirit of sons, and it makes us cry out, 'Abba, Father!' The Spirit himself and our spirit bear united witness that we are children of God. And if we are children we are heirs as well: heirs of God and coheirs with Christ, sharing his sufferings so as to share his glory" (Rom. 8:14-17).

This is authentic 'religious' or 'spiritual' formation, education, training or pedagogy because it is that of the Best Teacher or Pedagogue, who is God Himself.

Indeed, did not God himself reveal through the prophets – especially Jeremiah and Ezechiel that he would take the law that was written on tablets of stone and put it within our hears in a new dispensation of the new covenant, when he would give us 'a new heart and a new Spirit' – his own Spirit, that makes us 'free children of God'? (See Jeremiah 31:31-34; Ezechiel 11:17-20; 36:24-28).

> "Behold, days are coming," declares the LORD, "when I will make a new covenant with the house of Israel and with the house of Judah, not like the covenant which I made with their fathers in the day I took them by the hand to bring them out of the land of Egypt. They broke that covenant of mine so I had to show them who was master. It is Yahweh who speaks."

> "But this is the covenant which I will make with the house of Israel after those days," declares the Lord, "I will put my law within them, and on their heart I will write it; and I will be their God, and they shall be My people" (Jer. 31:31-33).

> "I am going to take you from among the nations and gather you together from all the foreign countries, and bring you home to your own land. I shall pour clean water over you and you will be cleansed; I shall cleanse you of all your defilement and all your idols. I shall give you a new heart, and put a new spirit in you; I shall remove the heart of stone from your bodies and give you a heart of flesh instead. I shall put my spirit in you, and make you keep my laws and sincerely respect my observances." (Ez. 36:31-34).

This 'interior law' is God's own Spirit, Jesus' Spirit, given to each of us, baptised in the Spirit in a personal way. It is a life-attitude which flows into actual, practical day-to-day living. It is this "new heart and new Spirit", which is a person's secret of inner freedom. No wonder, once discovered or discerned in depth, it impels a person from within to express himself or herself – that is, the person's truest and deepest self – in those very external exercises and practices that make up the day-to-day living out of Christian life. Only – and this is the vital, crucial difference! – no longer now as a cut-up fragmented discipline to which one submits from the 'outside' as it were, but as the expression of utter joyous freedom from within the core of one's authentic self.

If the 'Spirit' of God and of Jesus is at the heart of the Triune God already, the handing-over-of-the Father to the Son and the Son's response of handing over himself to the Father, namely, the mutual 'handing-over-of-self in love' – is it surprising that God's Spirit, Jesus' Spirit given to each one of us in a uniquely personal way is **each one's personal secret of handing-over-self-in-love**, i.e. each one's secret of being **authentically** a Christian, a **true disciple of Jesus Christ?**

PART 2
Context to grasp God's wonderous pedagogy in His all-wise plan of Redemption and Salvation

The History of the Patriarchs in Genesis, Chapters 12-50

After having related in the language of 'religious history' the origins of the world and of humanity, the author(s) of the Book of Genesis move on to gather together and weave into one narrative the many episodes that formed a fragmentary tradition concerning the 'patriarchs' or forbears of the people of Israel: Abraham, Isaac, Jacob and his twelve sons. The last of these sons, Joseph, merits a particular and almost entire biography, covering the final fourteen chapters (Chaps. 37-50) of the Book of Genesis, all because of his extraordinary adventure which records God's peculiar and wondrous way of seeing through his design and plan of love, redemption and salvation. The 'God of surprises' – "God's foolishness is wiser than human wisdom, God's weakness is stronger than human strength" (1 Cor. 1:25) – that 'God of surprises' who, in upsetting our 'worldly' values, shows that he is ever faithful to his loving design: in a word, the 'Mystery of the Cross', which is death and resurrection as **one mystery**.

It is the call of Abraham (Chap. 12) that marks the true beginning of the history of Israel – the chosen people, chosen to safeguard, in the midst of a corrupt and idolatrous world, the worship of the **one and only true God**. It is this 'choice', (or 'election') present 'in germ' (as in a seed) in the call of **Abraham**, which is concretised in an 'alliance' (or covenant). This takes a **definitive form** in the 'alliance' made on Mount Sinai, when **Moses** becomes God's instrument of 'choice' and 'covenant'.

These same themes of choice (election) and covenant (alliance) thereafter run through the narratives concerning **Isaac** and **Jacob**. The story of **Joseph** highlights especially the loving care and providence of God in leading to **fulfilment his own plan and design** – the unfailing care with which he surrounds his 'Chosen Ones'.

We must never forget that all these accounts and narrative are 'sacred history'. They are **not** meant to feed our curiosity about the scientific historical or geographical details; they are 'religious', 'sacred' in nature, to lead us to a relationship with a God of love, who guides and directs the course of history through its ups and downs to the fulfilment and completion of his own plan of liberating, redeeming and saving all of humankind and all of the cosmos – a plan conceived in love and carried out, step by step, pedagogically, **only in love**. Because it is all shot through with God's love through his Son Jesus and in their Spirit of love, God never imposes his plan or design of love on us, men and women. God calls us to **freely** and **responsibly** and **actively** receive and accept his loving design and collaborate with him, his Son and Spirit, in the working out of this, his plan and design.

It is worth noting that some of the passages of this 'History of the Patriarchs' – especially those pertaining to the principal source, known as the 'Yahwist' tradition – have an exceptional value **even a literary value**, because they combine deep religious sentiments with a keen sensitivity to colour, picturesque scenery, warmth and humanness, becoming themes themselves because of the traits of God's own life, love and peace.

Advent for Mary

From the very first moment Mary appears in the New Testament, in the mystery of the Annunciation (Lk. 1:26 ff), she is set forth as the 'model of faith'. It is God who breaks into Mary's life: Mary does not go to God; it is God who comes to Mary, taking the initiative of his saving and redeeming love. Addressed by the archangel Gabriel, in God's name, as "full of grace" or "highly favoured one", Mary is "greatly troubled": there must be some mistake here; she knows herself to be the simple, humble maidservant of the Lord. "Do not be afraid, Mary," she is reassured, as were Moses and the prophets of old, or later the apostles of the new dispensation; "it is you who have found favour with the Lord". And when she is further told that she "will conceive and bear a son who will be called the Son of the Most High", she does not jump to appropriate this role, which every young woman in Israel was longing for – to be the mother of the Messiah. In all truth and honesty, Mary seeks to clarify her real situation: "How can this be (that I have a son), since I have no relations with men?" Once again, she is reassured, in God's name, that God and God alone will do it all: "The Holy Spirit will come upon you, and the power of the Most High will overshadow you; therefore, the child that will be born of you will be called Son of God." Even **then**, Mary does not respond, as it were appropriating the gift of the Lord; she does **not** say anything like: "All right, then, I will be the Mother of the Incarnate Lord." Her only response is that of genuine faith, that of total availability to God as God, to God's call and vocation, from her real situation and accepting herself for who she is: "I am the maidservant of the Lord; let it be done to me – *not I shall do it* – according to your Word". With all the power and energy of her free will, Mary **let God be God** in her life; Mary gave God a real, serious chance in her life.

Again, in Mary's case – as in Abraham's – this initial attitude of the response of authentic faith to God's call of love is not merely the starting-point of her mystery. It is, in fact, the whole and entire mystery of Mary, lived out progressively and in every deepening fashion along the journey of her life and its real challenges, right up to the foot of the Cross.

Advent for us
"Have you not heard his silent steps?
He comes, comes, ever comes.
Every moment and every age,
Every day and every night

He comes, comes, ever comes.

> Many a song have I sung
> In many a mood of mind,
> But all their notes have always proclaimed
> He comes, comes, ever comes."

Rabindranath Tagore, Gitanjali

From the beginning to end, the Church in the season of Advent prays insistently for the coming of Jesus Christ as the fulfilment of our **HOPE:** *"Come, Lord Jesus!"* What coming of Christ are we praying for? If it is the birth of Christ, how can we still *look forward* to it, how *pray* for it? What meaning would such a 'hope'; have, since its object has already been realised in the past? This would be merely 'pious' play-acting! But the Church – and we **are** the Church – is really and seriously expressing in prayer an expectation of Christ who is still to come. If our Advent is deprived of this **real** "longing and yearning", it is emptied of its deep meaning and significance, of its realism and its living spiritual depth.

We must grasp that the Church is *training* us, through a **real** *"longing and yearning"*, for Christ who is still to come at the end of time to bring to a final fulfilment his Father's loving plan of liberation, salvation and redemption, when he will gather all of 'liberated creation' throughout the universe, to take it united with him to the Father, so that "God will be all in all" (1Cor. 15:28).

This longing for the future coming of Christ is an **essential** element in the true Christian spirit and outlook; because of this, the early Christians always met every week on a Saturday night, and spent the time in prayer and readings from the Scriptures: a 'watching or vigil' all night to celebrate the Eucharist in the early morning, as a *regular training* of the *heart* to 'look forward' to the real final coming of Jesus Christ.

So our **Advent** is a 'remembering' of the *past* coming of Christ in his incarnation and birth, to 'get ready' for the real *future* coming of him at the end of time. But, as a very good teacher, our mother Church, taught by her own Master Jesus Christ (the best of teachers), knows that we shall not be truly ready with open hearts for the future final coming of Jesus, unless we 'practise' *in the present* to keep our hearts open for the daily coming of Jesus Christ, who really comes to us in the persons, events and circumstances we meet every single day and every moment of every day. For, "He comes, comes, ever comes".

In a word, then, **Advent** is a *realistic training and preparation*: we 'remember' the past, to 'look forward' to the *future*, by 'practising' in the *present* to keep our hearts open for Him "who always comes". And, **all this very 'realistically' in the 'real'!**

Fr. Herbert Alphonso SJ

Additional Suggestions and Resources

> **Understand the meaning of Covenant.**
> **Reflect on some of the covenants God has made with us.**

Introduction

Explain to students that you will be taking them through an overview of the most significant events in salvation history up to the time of the birth of Jesus. With the help of Power Point Presentations you will be recapping on Creation and Noah, then Abraham, Moses, David, exile, prophets, advent, nativity and second coming of our Lord. The theme linking all the major events is God's faithfulness to his covenant.

In ancient times a covenant was an agreement or treaty between two people or two groups, often solemnised by a ceremony where both sides pledged assent to the obligations of the covenant. In the Hebrew Scriptures, the Old Testament, it mainly refers to the special relationship between Yahweh and Israel as the Chosen People of God. In the New Testament, it refers to the universal covenant established in the blood of Jesus Christ between God and the new people, the followers of Jesus.

Starting Point:

The concept of covenant needs to be carefully explained and a clear distinction made between a contract for a job or football player and a covenant. The text in the student's book will need to be demonstrated or it may help to use the flipcharts on the DVD.

Flipcharts: Covenant and Contract.

Assessment Folder: 'Contracts *benefit* but covenants *transform*'.

PPP: Creation and Noah.

Genesis 9:1-18 describes God's covenant with Noah after the flood. God renews the blessing of creation. It is a universal covenant, a binding treaty, not just with Noah and his descendants, but with all living things (Gen. 9:8-17). God is committed to life, to the continuance of life on earth, and whatever happens he will not let life disappear. Our part in the covenant is to take care of the non-human world: vegetable, animal, rainforests and the many species. The rainbow is a sign of God's covenant.

Assessment Folder: What should we remember when we experience or hear about extreme weather conditions?

 PPP: Abraham.

God makes a covenant with Abraham and his descendants. God promises that he will make Abraham the father of many nations. God promises to be the God of Abraham and his descendants.

Make links:

In order to give students an overview of salvation history it may be helpful to give a brief overview of the life of Joseph.

 PPP: Joseph.

Additional activity: Make an 'emotional graph' to show the 'highs' and the 'lows' in the life of Joseph.

> **God chose Moses to lead his people towards the Promised Land.**
> **Reflect on God's choice of leader.**

Starting Point:

Think about the ways in which God has been with Abraham and Joseph.

Allow a few minutes for students to reflect on challenging situations in their own lives and try to see how God has been with them. If you have time, you may wish to use the reflection 'Footprints'.

Invite students to tell you what they already know about Moses. Explain that they are now going to study the main events at a theological level to discover the message that God has for us today.

The Bible is the Word of God and it continually speaks to us when we make time to reflect on the scripture text.

Points for discussion:

Imagine you are an Israelite living as a slave in Egypt. What qualities would you look for in a leader to get you out of the country?

 PPP (Part 1): Moses. This may be useful to sum up the main events.

God calls Moses: Emphasise the key points:
- God takes the initiative to call Moses.
- Moses acknowledges God as God.
- He knows that the task he is being asked to do is too difficult.
- God promises to be with him.
- Moses believes that God will be faithful to his promise.

Additional activities

Choose a country or a group that needs to be freed from oppression today.

a) Write a job description for the leader of this campaign. Include:

- aims;
- challenges;
- qualities of leader.

b) Would you apply for this job? Give reasons.

Look again at your job description.

a) What would the difference be between the person you have described and Moses?

b) What would be the same?

c) Would Moses have got the job? Give reasons with reference to Ex. 3:7-10.

Slavery: In England, slavery was abolished after great efforts by William Wilberforce. Research the life and work of William Wilberforce and the work of the Abolition of Slavery Movement.

 Assessment Folder: Moses had difficulty believing he was the right man for the job God was asking him to do.

> **Know how Jews celebrate the Passover today.**
> **Reflect on the importance of this meal for Jewish families.**

Starting Point:

Invite students to share what they know about the major Christian festivals. If there are students of other faiths invite them to share as well.

Explain that the Passover is a major Jewish festival. It is also known as Pesach. Preparation for the Passover is found in Exodus 12:3-15. This command is taken seriously. The house is thoroughly cleaned before the Passover. They remember that their ancestors made bread without yeast so every trace of yeast is removed, not only in bread but in cakes and biscuits.

 ## WS 1 The Seder at our house.

Judaism: Websites to explain the four sons section of the Haggadah:
http://www.holidays.net/passover/four_sons.htm
http://www.angelfire.com/pa2/passover/thefoursons.html
http://www.chabad.org/holidays/passover/pesach_cdo/aid/467945/jewish/The-Educators-Handbook.htm - from the perspective of a parent towards each of the four sons

Quick quiz:

There are several bottles of wine on the table for the Passover meal. During the meal each person will drink four glasses of wine (or maybe just four sips) to remember the four promises God made to the Jews. What are the four promises? Read Exodus 6:6-7.

Answer:

I will free you from the Egyptians.

I will release you from slavery.

I will adopt you as my own people.

I will be your God.

Answer to activity page 34

Identify ways in which Christianity is lived out in the home.

The importance of a statue, holy picture, crucifix; saying grace before meals; morning and night prayers; the practise of forgiveness; making Sunday a holyday when the family go to Mass.

 Assessment Folder: The first Passover dates back to Moses about 3,000 year ago.

See BBC website World Religions for additional information on Judaism.

> ## Know about the Exodus.
> ## Reflect on the message it has for us today.

Starting Point:

Have you ever felt that the problems and burdens you have were too great? Without saying what the problem was, describe your feelings.

We can only imagine the burden of responsibility that Moses felt as he prepared to lead the Israelites out of Egypt. Trusting in God's word had enabled him to obtain permission from Pharaoh – the unknown was always before him – so he had to grow daily in his trust in God.

Differentiation: The summary of the exodus in the student's textbook is only intended as an overview or for the less able. Students should be asked to read the account of the Exodus in their Bible, (Ex. 13:17-22 and 14:1-31) and draw out the main key points to remember.

For homework students could be asked to read the account of the 'Manna and the Quails' (Ex. 16); and the 'Water from the Rock' (Ex. 17:1-7) and to make a summary to highlight how God is with his Chosen People.

 WS 2 The Israelites – Faith, Challenge, Blessing (Guided thinking map).

 Assessment Folder: Compare and contrast the people of the Exodus with refugees today.

 WS 3 Multiple Choice Quiz.

Note: The Ten Commandments has been covered in detail in Book 5 of this series for primary schools but the approach here is quite different.

Starting Point:

Why do we need rules? In what ways do our school rules help, in what ways do they hinder us. *If students say that their freedom is restricted by school rules, explain what true freedom really means.*

It was when the Israelites were wandering in the desert that God gave the commandments and it was these commandments that helped to give them a sense of identity. They are the people of the Law and that is still important to the Jews to this day. The wandering in the desert was also part of God's plan to build a nation dedicated to him from which would come the Messiah.

Audio recording: The Ten Commandments.

Flipcharts: The Commandments.

For activity 3 on page 39 'Choose any one of the Ten Commandments and prepare a '*Speech*'. Invite students to volunteer to give their speech. The class could agree on the three best speeches and these could be used as a basis for collective worship or a school assembly.

WS 4: The Ten Commandments (Guided thinking map).

WS 5: The Ten Commandments Today (In TB and on DVD ROM).

WS 6: Moses – Faith, Challenge, Blessing (Guided thinking map).

WS 7: A chart to show how the Decalogue is contained in the Great Commandment to love the Lord your God with all your heart and your neighbour as yourself.

Assessment Folder: four tasks.

Covenantal goods are non-zero-sum games – give examples.

The Ten Commandments are out of date. Discuss.

Which of the commandments could be applied to school life?

PPP part 2 Moses: this may be useful to summarise the main events.

WS 8 Crossword on Covenant.

> **Know that God sent prophets to remind the people
> of his covenant and unfailing love for them.
> Reflect on the message of the prophets for us today.**

Starting Point:

Invite students to describe the type of person they respect even though at times they may prevent them doing what they would like to do. What are the most important qualities they recognise in these people?

Explain that God wants what is best for us. When we pray, we may not get what we request at the time but very often when we look back on our lives we can see how everything has worked out best in the end.

 PPP: David – This Power Point will help to make links in the history of salvation leading up to Solomon. It can also be used to show how God was with David and when David sinned he sent the prophet Nathan to correct him.

 PPP: Solomon and Exile – This is to help students follow the plan of God in salvation history particularly in the section 'Promises Broken' on page 42. It may also help students to make links with the readings from the Old Testament which are used at Mass.

 Audio Recording: Jeremiah 31:31-33.

Activity page 43:

The prophet Ezekiel said that God will remove the heart of stone from our bodies and give us a new heart of flesh instead.

Compare and contrast the ideas in this prophecy. This could be in the form of a diagram of two hearts. You may need to give some prompts. For example, heart of stone: cold, unresponsive, no feelings for others; heart of flesh: life-giving, reaches out to others, loving.

 PPP: The Prophets.

 PPP: The Covenants.

 WS 9 Covenants.

 Assessment Folder: Prophets.

www.tere.org Go to Secondary and click on KS3 Support Material to find 'Prophets Covenant'.

> **Understand that Jesus has come and has made a New Covenant with us.**
> **Prepare to celebrate the birth of Jesus.**

Note: Remember to read the theological notes on Advent pages 32-33.

Starting Point:

For several weeks, we have studied how the Israelites escaped from slavery in Egypt and then led a life of faithfulness and unfaithfulness, gratitude and ingratitude. Now we need to reflect on our own passage from slavery to freedom.

 WS 10 use for reflection: 'Yet if His Majesty Our Sovereign Lord'.

 PPP: Advent.

Blessing of Advent Wreath

To prepare for the coming of Jesus Christ, the light of the world, we now bless this Advent Wreath and light the first of the candles which represent the four weeks of Advent.

Blessed are you, Lord, God of all creation.
In your great love you gave us Jesus your Son
to be our Saviour and to bring the light of grace into our world.

May this Advent Wreath be an every-present reminder of the
coming of Jesus that we may all renew our lives and become
worthy to be called his followers.

 PPP: The Annunciation.

Additional Activity:

In parts of mainland Europe, Christmas is celebrated by going to Mass and sharing as a family. Gifts are given on the feast of St. Nicholas (6th December) or the feast of the Epiphany (6th January).
a) Do you think this is a good idea? Give reasons for your answer.
b) Why do you think these particular feasts are chosen as 'gift-giving' days?
c) Gift-giving is an important feature of Judaism, Christianity, Islam and other faiths. What is so important about giving gifts?

 PPP: The Nativity.

 WS 11 'The Visit of the Magi'.

 Assessment Task: Happy Holiday or Happy Christmas

The Ten Commandments

Choose one of the Commandments. Use this diagram to show the impact it could have on:

- our own life;
- family, friends;
- the rest of society. [AT1 L4 (iii)]

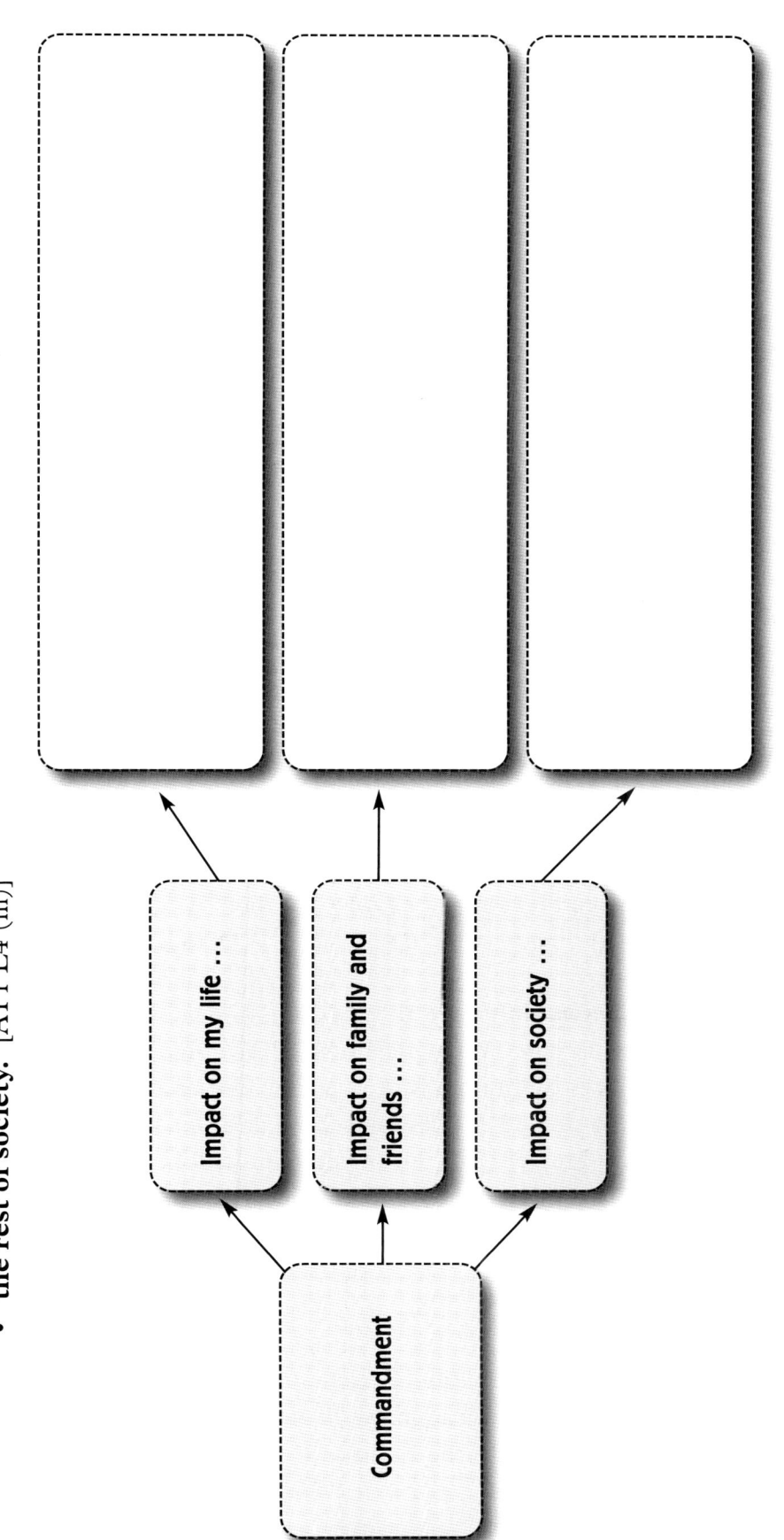

Impact on my life ...

Impact on family and friends ...

Impact on society ...

Commandment

Seder Night at our House

For me, Seder night just might be my favourite night (Jewishly!) of the year. Dad is busy moving all the furniture upstairs so that we can fit one long dining table through the house and squeeze as many people in as possible. Mum and whoever she can persuade to help, are in the kitchen all day, peeling mountains of potatoes, boiling pans of eggs, preparing all that is needed for the Seder plate and for the meal that comes halfway through the evening.

As evening approaches, the family arrive: grandparents, aunts, uncles, cousins, family friends who find themselves at a loose end this year. All stream into the house and find a space around the table. We sit back and recline as free people and prepare to recount the story of the exodus from Egypt, not as if it happened to our ancestors, but as if it were happening to us – for on Seder night we speak of how 'This is done because of that which the Lord did to me when I left Egypt (Exodus 13; 18)'. Throughout the Seder, we will drink four cups of wine, but tonight we do not pour our wine for ourselves because tonight we are free men. We pour for each other so that everyone can feel as if they now are free. We recline at the table to appreciate the luxuries of freedom.

In our family, the tradition is that we all take turns to read from the Haggadah aloud. When it gets to the Ma Nishtana (The Four Questions), the youngest child gets their starring role as they sing the questions to all present and everyone else responds with the answers. My four year old cousin has just started at a Jewish school and this year will be the first time he sings the Ma Nishtana all by himself. We're not sure who will be proudest – him, his Parents, his Grandparents or his Great-Grandma – all will be there to hear him! When it gets to the part about the Four Sons, my Dad will pick who gets to be the Wise, the Wicked, the Simple and the One that is too young to ask a question. Everyone is included; everyone takes part and shares in the evening.

The whole evening is all about audience participation. We are told to point at items on the Seder plate to explain their significance; we lift the Matza and declare that 'This is the bread of affliction which our fathers ate in the Land of Egypt. Let all who hunger come and eat. Let all who are in need come and partake of the Passover." We speak of the Ten Plagues that were set upon the Egyptians and, at the mention of each plague, we spill a drop of wine from our glasses with our finger as a reminder that whilst we rejoice at our freedom, we are sensitive to the suffering of the Egyptians, so our joy diminishes, if only in the mildest extent. We eat foods symbolic of the story of Pesach – bitter herbs to signify the bitterness of slavery, salt water to signify the tears of the slaves, charoset to represent the cement that they used when working for Pharaoh.

All of this is done in the knowledge that all across the country and across the world, families and friends are gathering together to share the same experience, with some of their own traditions thrown in. They have been doing so for thousands of years. It's an idea that I find hugely comforting and its part of the reason that Seder night grounds me so strongly into my Jewish identity and my connections with my history.

The Seder goes long into the night with prayers and stories and finishes with songs. Did you know that this is just the start? For the rest of the week whilst we don't gather for such a performance every night, we have the daily reminders in the food that we eat (which cannot be leavened) to keep the story of Pesach at the forefront of our minds.

Hannah Ashleigh

Activity

1. What are the most important aspects of the Seder for the Jews?

2. The Jews have been celebrating Passover for thousands of years.
   a) Why do you think they celebrate in this way?
   b) How do you think it helps them as:
      an individual;
      a family;
      a community?

3. Research:
   a) Find out about the Four Sons. This website will help you:
      http://www.holidays.net/passover/four_sons.htm
   b) Who does each son represent?
   c) In what sense is it true that we are all a little bit like each of the sons? Give examples.
   d) What lesson might we learn from the Four Sons?

8.3 Mystery of the Eucharist

Religious Education Curriculum Directory

"In the Eucharist we participate in the Lord's sacrifice. We are joined to the eternal praise and thanksgiving he offers as Son of the Father, and to his sacrifice on the cross. We receive him as our life and food, a promise of the eternal banquet of heaven. At the heart of the Eucharistic celebration are the bread and wine that become in reality Christ's Body and Blood. Catholic faith adores this enduring presence of Christ not only within the celebration of the Mass but also outside it." (p. 24)

Attainment Target 1: Learning *about* the Catholic faith.
Attainment Target 2: Learning *from* the Catholic faith.

Key Learning Objectives:

- Understand that Jesus is our Saviour.
  - Think about what this means for us.

- Know that Jesus is the Bread of Life.
  - Think about how it might affect your life.

- Understand the New Covenant that Jesus makes with us.
  - Reflect on our part in this New Covenant.

- Know that at the beginning of Mass, we ask for God's forgiveness for our sins.
  - Reflect on what this means.

- Know that the Bible is the Word of God.
  - Think of ways in which you can put the Word of God into practice.

- Understand what happens at the Offertory.
  - Reflect on how some people prepare to make their offering.

- Know that at the Consecration Jesus becomes truly present on the altar.
  - Think about what this means to you.

- Understand the sacrifice Jesus made for us.
  - Reflect on how we can participate in it.

- Know that when we receive Holy Communion, Jesus is truly present in the bread and wine.
  - Consider how we should prepare for this occasion.

- Reflect on how we can live out the Mass in our daily life.

- Understand that Jesus is sacramentally present in the Blessed Sacrament.
  - Reflect on how that can help us.

Theological Notes

THE EUCHARIST:
Source and Summit of all Christian Life and Activity

Part 1

From Jesus' promise of the Eucharist in Chapter 6 of St John's Gospel we gather the immense riches of this mystery. "Jesus said: 'I am the living bread which came down from heaven; if anyone eats of this bread, that person will live for ever; and the bread which I shall give for the life of the world is my flesh' The Jews then disputed among themselves, saying, 'How can this man give us his flesh to eat?'. So Jesus said to them, 'Truly, truly I say to you, unless you eat the flesh of the Son of Man and drink his blood, you have no life in you; the one who eats my flesh and drinks my blood has eternal life, and I will raise up that person at the last day. For my flesh is food indeed, and my blood is drink indeed. The one who eats my flesh and drinks my blood abides in me and I abide in that person. As the living Father sent me, and I live because of the Father, so the one who eats me will live because of me. This is the bread which came down from heaven, not such as the fathers ate and died: the one who eats the bread will live for ever'" (Jn.6:51-58).

This section alone of Jesus' discourse on "the bread of life", in which He promises the gift of the Eucharist, shows us how infinitely rich this mystery is – so rich, with so many precious facets to it, that we cannot take it all in at one glance as it were. We have to approach it from several angles, at different levels of depth. The Eucharist, we gather from this passage, is **a meal**, a true meal. When the Jews are shocked and scandalised at Jesus' words, taking it all for sheer 'cannibalism', Jesus does not backtrack on his words, offering some sort of metaphorical, figurative or symbolic interpretation of them. No: he repeats and emphasises that he means truly and really **his flesh and blood** as food and drink: "My flesh is **real food**, my blood is **real drink**." So the Eucharist is a real and true meal, but not any kind of meal. It is a **sacrificial meal**: "the bread that I shall give is my flesh given for the life of the world". It is the body of Jesus Christ offered out of love as a **sacrifice of expiation**, a sacrifice that takes our sins away, which is eaten in this meal; a **sacrifice of communion**, too, for Jesus says: "The one who eats my flesh and drinks my blood abides in me, and I abide in that person". It is the "bread of life", of eternal life: "the one who eats this bread will live for ever". If we were to add to all of this other scriptural prefigurings and foreshadowings of the Eucharist, such as we have for example in Chapters 12, 13 and 24 of the Book of Exodus, we see that the Eucharist is a meal connected with a 'memorial sacrifice' (Ex. 12-13), 'memorial' of the passage from slavery to freedom, from death to life, a meal connected indeed with the 'covenant sacrifice' of Mt. Sinai (Ex. 24), now the 'new covenant' in the blood of Jesus Christ. So many varied and diversified aspects of the infinitely rich mystery of the Eucharist!

And yet, the most fundamental and profound aspect, the one which lies at the basis of, and gives vital meaning to, every other aspect of this infinitely rich mystery is what we will explore in this module. It shines forth resplendently in St Paul's account of the institution of the Holy Eucharist, such as we have it recorded in his First Letter to the Corinthians.

"For I received from the Lord what I also delivered to you, that the Lord Jesus on the night when he was betrayed took bread, and when he had given thanks, he broke it, and said, 'This is my body which is for you. Do this in remembrance of me'. In the same way also the cup, after supper, saying, 'This cup is the new covenant in my blood. Do this, as often as you drink it, in remembrance of me'. For as often as you eat this bread and drink the cup, you proclaim the Lord's death until he comes."
(1 Cor.11: 23-26)

This Pauline institution narrative, according to the Greek original, actually says the following: "For I received from the Lord what I also **handed over to you**, that the Lord Jesus on the night when **he was handed over**, took the bread, and when he had given thanks, he broke it and said, 'This is my body which is **handed over** for you. Do this in remembrance of me'." The repetition of the verb 'handed over' is not just chance usage, no mere play upon words. It is one of St Paul's most favourite words, as we shall soon see, in the Greek *paradidomi*. So what Paul is saying is that what he received from the Lord, he has **handed over** to the Corinthian community - namely, that on the very night when the Lord was handed over in a betrayal of love, he, the Lord, in an ecstasy of love, took bread, gave thanks, broke the bread and said, "This is my body which is **handed over** for you. Do **this** in remembrance of me".

By using these words 'handed over', St Paul, passionate lover of Jesus Christ, offers us, under the inspiration of the Spirit, the singularly deep and crucially characteristic meaning of the Eucharist and its mystery. In this profoundly rich and realistic aspect of the Eucharist, every other aspect of which we have spoken earlier, takes on its true and authentic significance, assumes its genuine value and importance. Here it is, in the 'handing over of self in love', that we grasp what kind of 'meal' the Eucharist is.

St Paul has, in fact, 'handed over' to us and to all generations of Christians the profound **realism** of the Eucharist, that **realism** which makes the Eucharist and its mystery the hub-centre of the whole sweep of Christian life and activity. As Vatican II in its Constitution on the Sacred Liturgy significantly phrases it, 'the source and summit of all Christian life and activity' *(Sacrosanctum Concillium 10)*. It is Paul's institution narrative that reveals to us the realism of Jesus' injunction, "Do **this** in remembrance of me". Jesus is not asking his disciples and us his followers merely 'to consecrate bread and wine' in remembrance of him. Not at all! What Jesus is saying is: **"Do this, which I have done, in remembrance of me"** – that is, while consecrating bread and wine, as I have done, **hand over yourselves in love, as I have done.** This is the memorial; this is the remembrance in action of Jesus and of what he did for us.

We could well ask ourselves why it is that we have, in recent times, tended to water down **this profound realism** of the Eucharist which is actually its core meaning and far reaching significance. Is this because we have tended to water down the realism and mystery of redemption?

I cannot forget that when I studied my theology in the late fifties and early sixties (1957-61), just before Vatican II, the categories that tended to be emphasised in the theology of redemption were more 'juridical' in character rather than truly 'theological' categories that eventually watered down the 'realism' of redemption and the redemptive mystery. For instance, it was repeatedly impressed upon us that Jesus 'paid a ransom' to redeem us, the 'ransom' and 'price' of his precious blood to free us. Now, what we pick up from such a juridical category as 'ransom' is that if the 'ransom' is paid, we the 'prisoners' and 'captives' go scot-free; we have nothing more to do, no more responsibility, for we are already 'ransomed', 'redeemed'. Another juridical category offered to us in the 'theology of redemption' was that of 'vicarious satisfaction': in other words, Jesus **took our place** ('vicarious') in 'satisfying' for the sins and offences done to God by us sinners. Now if Jesus **took our place** was our 'Vicar', then we once again conclude that we go scot-free, that we have no more to do; the 'satisfaction' or making up of our sins has been done by Jesus.

Such a 'theology' (!) of redemption just does not square with what the word of God teaches us both about 'sin' and 'redemption from sin'; it simply does not concur with the 'stark realism' of the biblical witness. Actually, and very realistically, for **me** a sinner, no one can take **my** place in redemption – not even Jesus! Sin, for me a sinner, is **not** somewhere out there; sin is **in** me. For the core and essence of 'sin' is selfishness – my self-love, self-will and self-interest, which closes myself upon myself, which closes my heart to God who is constantly coming to me with his love, his life, indeed himself... Does this mean that Jesus did not do something irreplaceable in redeeming me, in redeeming all of us? Of course **he did**. And it is precisely in what he did to be truly 'our Redeemer', that we see wondrously focussed, the 'stark realism' of redemption. This, in fact, is the very burden of the Letter to the Hebrews on the 'priesthood of Jesus Christ', especially in chapters 9 and 10. The 'newness' of the 'new' priesthood of the 'new covenant' inaugurated by Jesus lies in the fact that Jesus did not, as did the high priest of the old covenant, enter year after year into the Holy of Holies with the blood of animals. "Jesus entered once for all into the holy place taking not the blood of goats and calves but his own blood, thus securing an eternal redemption." (Heb. 9:12)

It is, as we can clearly perceive, in **'handing over himself'** – his **own** flesh and blood – that Jesus opened a **new way**. In this he did something 'irreplaceable'; the way to the Father for us sinners was closed because of our selfishness and sin; in his own flesh Jesus opened a 'new way' so that we then each one of us, could walk that way of 'handing over self'. We begin to grasp, I hope, the very deep significance of Jesus' words: "I am the way...." (Jn. 14:16). What Jesus did for us irreplaceably as our unique Redeemer and Saviour, we are today calling 'objective redemption'. What we, each of us, who has already been objectively redeemed, have the free and irreplaceable responsibility of still doing, we are today calling 'subjective redemption' in a word, 'handing over ourselves in love'.

This, then, is the heart of the Eucharist and the mystery of the Eucharist: handing over self in love. We cannot celebrate the Eucharist authentically, unless we bring as the 'matter' and 'material' of our

Eucharist our real and realistic handing over of ourselves in our daily life, our personal life, our family life, our professional or work life, our social life, all our real life and living. As St. Augustine warns in one of his great sermons on the Eucharist, unless we are bringing to our Eucharistic celebration the realism of our daily gift and surrender of self, that is, of our handing over ourselves, we are **not** celebrating Eucharist: we are, he says, 'perpetrating one big lie'. For to be truly a Christian, truly a disciple of Jesus Christ, is to 'hand over self'. As Jesus one day said in lapidary fashion: "If anyone will come after me (that is, be my disciple) that person must renounce self, take up his/her own cross and follow me" (Mt. 16:24). This is not a tripartite criterion for authentic discipleship: it is a threefold expression of one single criterion: the gift and surrender of self or, in Pauline language, **the handing over of self**. No wonder St Paul sees in this 'handing over of self' the characteristic trait of Jesus' spirit, of **his** kind of loving. Twice in his Letter to the Ephesians he returns to it: "Christ loved us and **handed himself over for us**, a fragrant offering and sacrifice to God" (Eph. 5:2); and again: "Husbands, love your wives, as Christ loved the Church and handed **himself over for her**" (Eph.5:25). But Paul does not seem satisfied with speaking of Christ's love and kind of loving in general, for the Church or for all of us. His is a deeply **personal**, living and intimate relationship with Jesus: in his letter to the Galatians, he unabashedly professes: "I live, now not I but Christ lives in me; the life I now live, I live by faith in the Son of God who loved **me** and **handed himself over for me"** (Gal. 2:20).

Now perhaps, we understand why the Eucharist is the great sacrament that both signifies and effects 'unity and community'. If, as we know by daily experience, the biggest obstacle among us human beings to unity and community, what indeed destroys unity and community, is our human selfishness and self-sufficiency, then we understand that it is precisely our getting out of our selfishness, our handing over ourselves in love, which, on our part, creates and builds up 'unity' and 'community'. Radically and fundamentally, it was Jesus' handing over of himself in love in his paschal mystery that made him a living and life-giving Spirit (cf. 1 Cor. 5:45), open to everyone else, not closed in on himself, in other words, the basic and fundamental key to the 'unity' and 'community' of the Body of Christ which is the Church.

We have long been used to saying and repeating – and it is certainly true – that **the Church makes the Eucharist** in obedience to her Lord and Master's injunction at the Last Supper: "Do this in remembrance of me". But it is even more profoundly and significantly true **that the Eucharist makes the Church**. We need to dwell long on this, in order to grasp for real daily living, the intimate and organic relationship between the mystery of the Church and the mystery of the Eucharist. In a singularly and astonishingly profound sense, the Church makes the Eucharist and the Eucharist makes the Church. For it is only the realistic 'handing over of self in love' of the members of the Body of Christ which is the Church, that is the 'matter' which, empowered by the Head's own handing over of self in love, truly makes the Eucharist. It is the Eucharist then, binding together the Head and the members of the Body in close 'communion' and 'unity' through the gift of the Spirit and surrender of self, which makes the Church. Here it is that we have a privileged insight into the Vatican II statement in its Constitution on the Sacred Liturgy (n.10), designating the Eucharist as at once "the source and summit of all Christian life and activity". The 'summit' or peak to which the Church brings all of its life and activity is characteristically summed up in its day-to-day 'handing over of self in love'. At the same time, the 'source' or foundation from which the Church draws the strength and energy to be authentically in its daily life and activity the Church or Body of Christ, is recognised distinctively by its "fellowship and unity" in love precisely because of its 'handing over self in love'.

Indeed, the Church cannot be truly Church without the Eucharist. It is amazingly instructive to trace this in the course of history. Limiting ourselves here to the times of persecution – namely, the times when the Church was being 'handed over' as it were in her flesh by her enemies who sought to wipe her out of existence – we see how she strove and made every effort to celebrate the Eucharist, for she cannot exist without the Eucharist. So, when Roman emperors sought to persecute and destroy her, she went underground into catacombs to celebrate the Eucharist so that she could live and continue to live; she could not be the Church without the Eucharist. So, too, in the England of Queen Elizabeth 1: when the Church was hounded down, her hunted priests and their scattered flocks would scout out the most unlikely places like ramshackle and dilapidated barns to have the Eucharist, to celebrate Holy Mass. "It is the Mass that matters" became the defiantly-trumpeted slogan of those hounded-down Catholics, that persecuted Church. And in our own times, in Communist China in the 1950s and beyond, the persecuted priests with their flocks were doing exactly the same: going into hiding, going underground to celebrate the Eucharist, for the Church cannot survive without the Eucharist. One has only to read the heart-throbbing account of Father Lefure on the Catholics of Shanghai entitled "Les Enfants dans la Ville" (The Children in the City), to realise how right up to our times, resplendent witness is being borne to the enduring truth that the Eucharist expresses the very essence of the mystery of the Church. For the Church's very survival, for her everyday life and activity, "it is the Mass that matters".

To celebrate the Eucharist, then, is no mere ritual ceremony for which we, the Church, come together from time to time or even daily. In all its rich and profound realism, to celebrate the Eucharist is **faithfully to live out** the 'handing over of self in love' in the realistic struggles and battles of the arena of everyday living no less than in its real-life joys and consolations. The great St Francis de Sales, Bishop of Geneva, grasped this in practice: when busy during the day in his office on being asked once by a close associate what he was doing, Francis replied without batting an eyelid: "I am celebrating Mass!" "Celebrating Mass?" queried the associate, "you are poring over that book in front of you!" "Yes", reiterated Francis calmly, "I am celebrating Mass! For I **am** trying to live out in reality what I 'celebrated' sacramentally this morning".

We need to realise and assimilate the truth that once Jesus Christ 'handed himself over in love' for us in his Paschal Mystery, he remains forever eternalised in this act of handing self over. The Risen Jesus, as he lives today in the Church and in the world, is not Jesus as at any moment of his existence – a kind of 'generic' or 'general' Jesus. No! He carries forever 'stamped' on and in his person his 'handing over of self in love'. This is the meaning of what we have got so used to calling, 'the Risen Jesus with his glorious wounds'. This is, in fact, how St John in the Book of Revelations, sees the glorious Risen Lord while contemplating in awe 'the Divine Majesty surrounded by the heavenly Church'. "And between the throne and the four living creatures and among the elders, I saw a **Lamb standing, as though slain....**" (Rev. 5:6). The person of Jesus, then, with whom we are in a relationship of faith and love, whether as individual persons or as a community, is **this** Jesus as forever 'handed over in love'. So, too, is Jesus, as he is perpetually present in the Blessed Sacrament: having become present on our altars, during the celebration of the Eucharist, in the very act of 'handing himself over', he remains for us perpetually present in our tabernacles in the very same way; eternally handing himself over in love. One could hardly exaggerate the far-reaching significance of this. The Lord's love for us has been so exquisitely passionate and provident that, knowing how much and how constantly we would need to be fed and nourished on this **his** 'handing over of self in love' for **our own** daily 'handing over ourselves in love', he has remained for us **always** thus: giving and handing himself over in love for us. Here then we begin to grasp the profound theological meaning of what we are accustomed to call 'visits to the Blessed Sacrament'.

All we have thus far said about the inner meaning of Eucharist – that is, **the handing over of self in love** – entering into every area and details of our daily Christian life and activity, can finally be further confirmed by a word which, as Christians, we pronounce innumerable times almost mechanically every day. The word is "Amen"; and I wish to focus on it precisely within the context of the celebration of the Eucharist. At communion time, the priest or Eucharistic minister offers us the Body and/or the Blood of Christ with the words: "The Body and/or the Blood of Christ"; and we in receiving communion respond: "Amen". We have long been instructed that 'Amen' means 'so be it'; accordingly, we interpret **this** 'Amen' as equivalent to: 'I believe this is truly the Body and/or the blood of Christ, not just a piece of bread or just the wine I sip from the cup'. Actually the Hebrew word 'Amen' stems from the root 'emet' which signifies literally 'firm' or 'unshakeable' as a rock, and so stands for 'fidelity', committed faithfulness. So, what we are truly responding with an 'Amen' is that we mean to be 'faithfully committed' in real daily living to the mystery we are receiving – **faithfully committed' to living out our 'handing over self in love'** in our real daily living. In other words, our reception of what we call 'holy communion' is really, through the 'Amen' we pronounce, a serious and responsible commitment to faithfully living out in reality that which we are being fed and nourished on: the 'handing over self in love' which is, in deep truth, the mystery of 'communion' or unity, fellowship and community, as we have earlier shown. In this very profound sense, we do not just 'receive' holy communion; in deed and in truth, we 'become' holy communion or, at any rate, we seriously commit ourselves to 'becoming' in real daily living true 'communion', the holy 'common union' of Christian fellowship, unity and community. We can certainly understand, then, why St Augustine, in that same great sermon on the Eucharist I mentioned earlier on, urges the congregation at Mass to shout out its solemn 'Amen' at the doxology which concludes the Eucharist Prayer: "Through Him, with Him, in Him, in the unity of the Holy Spirit, all glory and honour is yours, Almighty Father, for ever and ever, **Amen**". In St Augustine's pressing invitation then, we perceive that in proclaiming loudly and in unison our 'Amen', we as the People of God, the Church, are committing ourselves in responsible faithfulness to living out the entire paschal mystery that we both prayerfully spelt out and made really present in mystery in the course of the Eucharistic Prayer – the mystery, that is, of handing over self in love together with Jesus Christ in the power of the Spirit to the glory of God the Father.

To conclude this section on the core-understanding of the Eucharistic mystery inspired in God's holy Word, we can do no better than recall than the deeply significant exhortation which the ordaining Bishop addressed to me and my companions many years ago in the solemn ceremony ordaining all 35 of us priests: *Agnoscite quod agitis; imitamini quod tractatis* – that is "Recognise what you are doing; imitate the mystery you are handling". This truly gets, as you surely notice, to the very heart of priestly existence so intimately connected with the Eucharistic mystery, that is, the mystery of **handing over self in love**. Each one of us is a priest, my priesthood is only and fully a service to your more fundamental and more radical Christian priesthood, for every baptised Christian is truly a priest, in the one and only priesthood of Jesus Christ. My **ordained, ministerial** priesthood is meant to be, in its entire sweep of life and activity, a service to your priesthood. To you, then, real priests, I would like to repeat that very exhortation which the ordaining Bishop addressed to me on the day of my Priestly Ordination: To you I say: "Recognise what you are doing when you celebrate Mass; imitate the mystery you are handling and receiving... Live out, that is, the heart of the realism of the mystery of the Eucharist: the mystery of **handing over yourselves in love** in your daily life and activity.

Fr. Herbert Alphonso SJ

Additional Suggestions and Resources

> **Understand that Jesus is our Saviour.**
> **Think about what this means for us.**

Note: It is essential for the teacher to have studied and reflected on the theological notes for this module before teaching it. There are more key learning objectives than in the other modules. You will probably cover one in each lesson.

Starting Point:

Why do you think this section of the book is called the 'Mystery of the Eucharist'? What is a mystery? What meaning is given in your textbook?

Do any of you know why we are going to start off with the account of Jesus feeding the five thousand men? What might the connection be with the Eucharist?

Explain that these lessons are going to be challenging. They will require us to be open to a new way of thinking that is, thinking theologically. We will be required to think in a deeper way and look for meanings that are not immediately obvious.

Let us imagine we are with the people on the hillside and let us take time to carefully 'think through' what Jesus is saying to the people and to us.

Additional Resources: Key Words and meanings. Students could learn these for homework. See suggestions for 'starters' in Tips for Teaching and Learning page 7 for ways to test their knowledge of them.

 Assessment Folder: Activity 2 page 49.

Songs: 'Open Our Eyes', CD How Can We Keep From Singing.
'Father I Have Sinned', CD And Again I Say Rejoice
CJM Music www.cjmmusic.com

> ## Know that Jesus is the Bread of Life.
> ## Think about how it might affect your life.

Starting Point:

It is essential to create the right atmosphere for quiet reflection before starting this lesson. You may like to light a candle and play some soft music just to help students settle down.

PPP: Sign of the Cross

Ask the students to silently reflect on what Jesus said: 'I am the bread of life ...' Jn. 6-35-36. Invite them to imagine they are with Jesus and write down the questions they would like to ask him.

PPP: Pope Benedict XVI explains "I am the bread of life".

Respond to questions: It is very important for the teacher to take time to thoughtfully respond to questions. We have to accept and respect those with no belief in the Eucharist and just encourage them to allow God to come to them in his own time.

Assessment Folder: 'I am the bread of life'.

> ## Understand the New Covenant that Jesus makes with us.
> ## Reflect on our part in this New Covenant.

Starting Point:

Ask the students what they remember about the prophecy of Jeremiah (Jer. 31:31-33) and Ezekiel (Ezek. 36:24-27; 31-34) on page 43 of textbook.

Flipchart: New Covenant.

Audio Recording: A New Commandment (Jn. 14).

WS 1: A New Commandment (Guided thinking map).

Assessment Folder: 'Look after yourself; nobody else will'. Discuss.

> ## Know that at the beginning of Mass we ask for God's forgiveness for our sins. Reflect on what this means.

Starting Point:
Ask students to give reasons why they go to Mass or why they should go to Mass.

 WS 2: Why go to Mass – some students reasons.
You may wish to project this onto the whiteboard and use it for discussion or give it to students as a worksheet and ask them to number them in the order of importance.

 Flipchart: Reasons for going to Mass.

 WS 3: Signs and Symbols at Mass.

 Flipchart: Signs and Symbols.

 WS 4: Overview of the Mass.
Worksheets 3 and 4 will help to give you some idea of what students already know about the Mass.

 Flipchart: Penitential Rite.

 PPP: Pope Benedict XVI – Why go to Mass?

To conclude: Invite students to share what has touched them most in this section and what they want to remember. What can they do to make sure the most important message stays with them? www.tere.org Go to 'Secondary' K3 Support Material to find 'MassExplained'.

> ## Know that the Bible is the Word of God. Think of ways in which you can put the Word of God into practice.

Starting Point:
What happens when you listen to someone speaking?
Does it matter who it is? Why?
Does it matter what they say? Why?
What would happen if God spoke to you? Why?

Allow the students to experience the Word of God: Explain that the Bible is God's Word.
When we are reflecting and meditating on a scripture text God is speaking to us through it. You may wish to give students a few lines, e.g.
"Do not let your hearts be troubled.
Trust in God still, and trust in me" (Jn. 14:1).

Other Resources on DVD: Psalm 23 and a reflection on Psalm 23.

In the reflection, ask students to identify the difference between the famous actor who recited the psalm and the old priest. *The actor knew the words of the psalm and recited them impressively but for the priest, the words of God had entered his heart – he truly believed them.*

It will be the same for the teacher in the classroom. If you make time to meditate on the scripture texts before you share them with the students the Word of God will *come alive* and have meaning and purpose for them.

 ### Flipchart: Liturgy of the Word.

Mass in school: try to make time for the students to meditate on at least one of the scripture texts before Mass is celebrated.

Sunday Mass: You may wish to choose one or two verses from one of the readings for Sunday Mass each week for reflection in order to help students find meaning and purpose in them.

> ## Understand what happens at the Offertory.
> ## Reflect on how some people prepare to make their offering.

Starting Point:

Invite the students to take time to reflect on what they do when they go to Mass. They do not need to share their thoughts.

Explain that we do not go to Mass as spectators but to actively participate in it. Invite suggestions on how to do it for the following:

Penitential Rite: *(We ask God's forgiveness for what we have done wrong and the grace to be ready to forgive others).*

Liturgy of the Word: *(We listen with our hearts and minds to a word or a phrase that God's really wants us to understand, for example, a word of comfort or encouragement).*

The Offertory: *(We make an offering of ourselves and all that we do to Jesus). See WS 6 on DVD ROM to use as a plenary to recap on ways to participate at Mass.*

Homework: Invite students to live as a fully committed follower of Jesus and to write down what they did and describe how they felt afterwards. Explain that this is part of the offering people make at the Offertory of the Mass. We offer all that we are and the efforts we make to love one another, to Jesus. Jesus unites our offering with his to the Father.

 ### Flipchart: The Offertory.

 **Assessment Folder:** Assessment task.

> **Know that at the Consecration, Jesus become truly present on the altar. Think about what this means for you.**

Note: In preparation for this lesson, it is important to re-read the first three pages of the theological notes on the Eucharist.

Starting Point:

Find out what students understand about the Consecration. Explain that you are now going to give them a much deeper understanding of the meaning.

You are going back in time to the Last Supper that Jesus had with the twelve disciples before he died.

When Jesus took the bread and wine, blessed it and gave it to the disciples he said, **"Do this in remembrance of me".** But Jesus was not asking his disciples and us, his followers, merely "to consecrate bread and wine" in remembrance of him. What Jesus is saying is: **"Do this, which I have done, in remembrance of me"** – that is, while consecrating bread and wine, as I have done, hand over yourselves in love, as I have done. This is the memorial; this is the remembrance in action of Jesus and of what he did for us.

Jesus handed over his life out of love for us. He gave his life for us and asks us to be willing to give our lives for him and for one another. In other words, Jesus was saying **'Do what I am doing out of love for me and for one another'.**

What does this mean? It means that during each day we strive to let go of self-love, self-will, self-pity. We ask Jesus for his help and with HIS help we can help others.

 ### Pause to reflect:

What happens at the Consecration of the Mass? Jesus is truly present. What can we do to help us grasp this extraordinary reality?

We have Jesus, really and truly present in the Blessed Sacrament in our Catholic churches. Have we become complacent? Do we truly believe it?

 PPP: Pope Benedict – Eucharist.

Flipchart: Consecration.

PPP: The Last Supper. It is essential to choose a time when students are most receptive for this PPP. It will help if the blinds are drawn and a quiet atmosphere has been created. Encourage the students to imagine they are there and allow time for them to stay with the images.

 PPP: The Lamb of God.

 PPP: Maximilian Kolbe (Student's Book page 66).

Reflect on how we can live out the Mass in our daily lives.

Starting point:

Invite students to explain why we do not go to Mass to observe what is happening but to participate in it.

 WS 6: Five ways to participate in the Mass. This can be used as a plenary and for less able students as an assessment task (Level 5).

 Assessment Folder - Assessment Task:

"The Mass is our Catholic Faith in a nutshell. What happened over 2,000 years ago is made present in the Mass today." Explain with reference to

- the Liturgy of the Word;
- the Offertory,
- the Consecration;
- Jesus' sacrifice;
- Holy Communion.

To obtain a Level 7 students will need to support their answer with reference to a variety of sources and evidence, e.g. Bible and Catechism of the Catholic Church or Compendium: Catechism of the Catholic Church. They may also use the textbook for reference but not to copy straight from it.

 PPP: The Catechism of the Catholic Church: How to use it. For the worksheet on page 59, show students how to look up a reference in the Catechism and encourage 'more able' students to use it.

The New Commandment
John 15:12

What is the new Commandment? Write it in the box on the left.

Explain how living this new Commandment could inspire you and other people to make your school a better place.

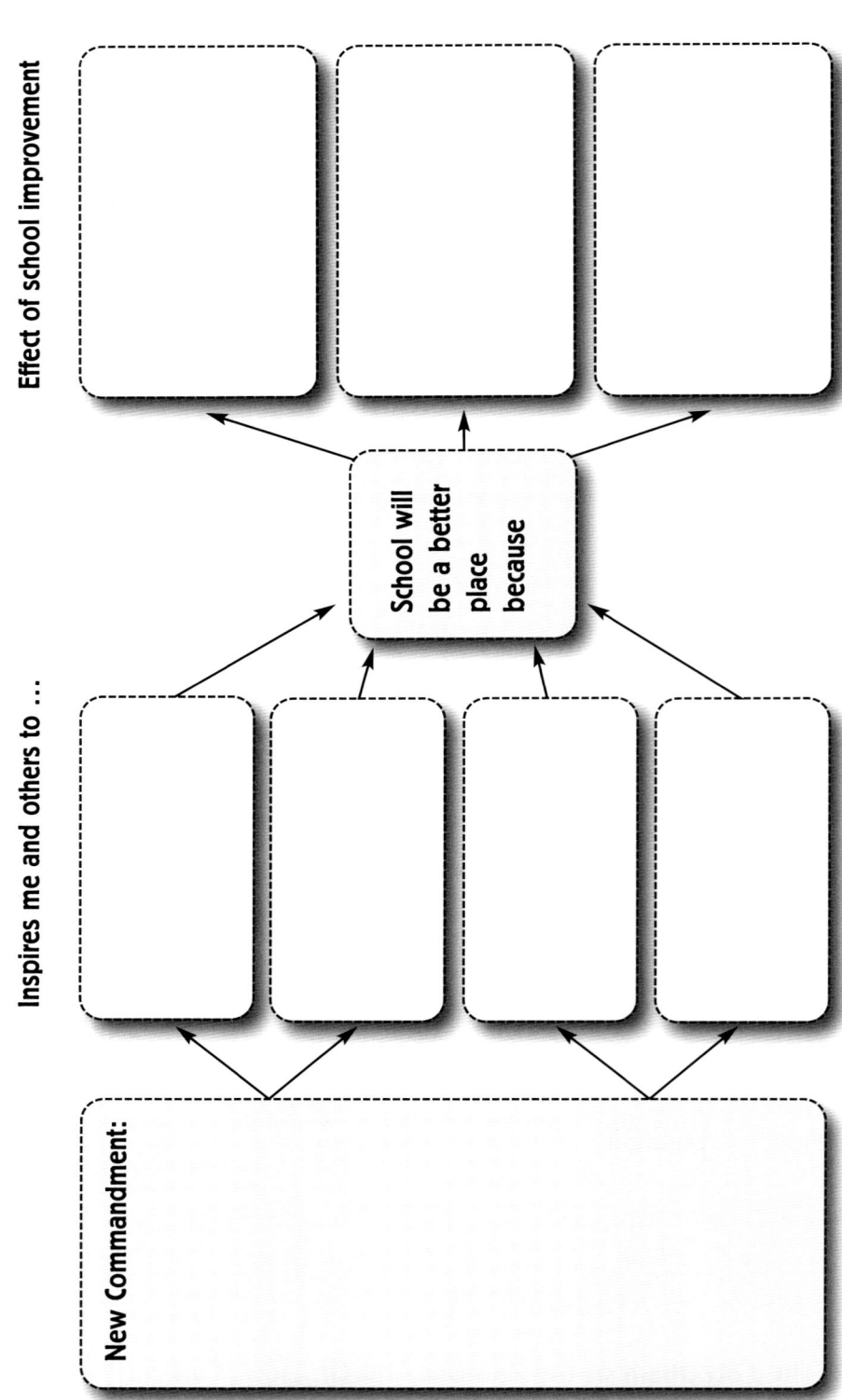

Effect of school improvement

Inspires me and others to …

School will be a better place because

New Commandment:

The Blessed Sacrament

Jesus promised to be with his Church 'until the end of time' (Mt. 28:20). One of the ways in which he fulfils this promise is through his abiding (permanent) presence in the Blessed Sacrament.

The Blessed Sacrament is the name we give to the consecrated hosts which are kept in the tabernacle so that we can always pray in the presence of Jesus. When we have Benediction the host is placed on the altar in a monstrance. Benediction is a special time of prayer, of adoring Jesus in the Blessed Sacrament.

The continuing presence of Jesus in the Blessed Sacrament is very special to all Catholic churches. This presence makes them a place of prayer and contemplation. It is what makes our churches a place of consolation and wonder. The sanctuary light tells us that Jesus is present in the tabernacle. We genuflect as a sign of respect.

"The Church and the world have a great need for Eucharistic worship. Jesus awaits us in the sacrament of love. Let us not refuse the time to go to meet him in adoration, in contemplation full of the faith, and open to making amends for the serious crimes of the world. Let our adoration never cease." (John Paul II, Dominicae cenae 3, cf. Catechism 1380).

Making a visit to the Blessed Sacrament
- Jesus has been waiting for us. He knows us.
- We allow time for our heart and mind to become conscious of the presence of Jesus in the tabernacle.
- We share with Jesus in a deeper way than we could ever share with anyone else. We can trust him.
- We can tell him everything.
- Slowly, surely, if we wait, peace will come over us.
- If we are trying to make a decision, we ask ourselves what Jesus would do if he were in this situation.

We recall the words of Jesus:
**"Do not let your hearts be troubled or afraid,
Trust in God still and trust in me"** (Jn. 14:1).

 **Activity**

1. a) What is the Blessed Sacrament?
   b) Why do we have the Blessed Sacrament in our churches?
   c) How do we know the Blessed Sacrament is present in a Catholic church?

2. 'We are never less alone than when we are alone with God.' Discuss.
   - Say what you **think** and **why**.
   - Give a different point of view and say why some people hold it.
   - Say why you **disagree** with it.
   - Quote some source of evidence.

3. Design a notice for outside the chapel or church door to explain to people that Jesus Christ is truly present in the Blessed Sacrament. For information read CCC 1377, 1378.

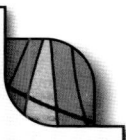

8.4 The Paschal Mystery

Theological Notes

8.4 The Paschal Mystery

It is here that we make the connection with the **Eucharistic Mystery** and the **new covenant.** At the Last Supper, Jesus changed the Jewish paschal meal from the offering of an external sacrifice – an animal, the paschal lamb – to the offering and **handing over of himself in love**. This is the radical change from the **old** covenant to the **new** covenant – not the blood of an animal (a lamb or goat or calf or heifer) but **his own blood** (Jesus' blood): "This cup **is the new covenant in my blood**" … **"the blood of the new and everlasting covenant …."** It is certainly striking how the Church, with a profoundly Christian instinct, on Holy Thursday – the day we celebrate the Institution of the Eucharist and of the Christian Priesthood – chooses for its Solemn Liturgy the gospel of the **Washing of the Feet** (Jn. 13:1-15). This is **not** the lesson merely of humble, selfless service **but the entire** DRAMA OF REDEMPTION, exactly parallel to the mystery of Christ's self-emptying, self-gift and self-surrender in love of CROSS AND RESURRECTION in the Pauline hymn **Philippines 2:5-11**. It is also in the second reading from **1 Corinthians 11: 23-26** which is Paul's account of the Institution of the Eucharist (**all** are centred on the Greek verb which means handing-over self).

At the Last Supper Jesus, with his heart full of love, opened that heart and shared with his beloved disciples and, through them, with all of us who were going to be his disciples down the centuries, his promise of pouring out his own Spirit. When his disciples were distraught at the fact that he was going to leave them, he assured and reassured them: "I must go. If I do not go, I cannot send the Spirit. I must go so that I can send the Spirit" (cf. Jn. 14:27-28; 16:6-7).

As disciples of Jesus Christ, we all have to go through our own Paschal Mystery. We shall have our own way of the cross. Certainly, that is never the end of the road: there is, in Christ Jesus, resurrection for each of us too. We shall experience the power of Christ's resurrection. But while we are on the road carrying the cross, we need the comfort, counsel and consolation which the Spirit of God will give us. He will be our friend, our comfort and our consolation. The Spirit will be our advocate not only before God, but before men and women who will resist and oppose God's call and work of salvation. The Spirit will be the one who will speak for us as our 'Advocate'. We recall Jesus telling his disciples: "You will be brought before courts and judges. Do not worry about what you have got to say. If you trust in the Lord, the Spirit of God himself will be speaking through your lips" (cf. Mk. 13:9-11; Mt. 10:17-20; Lk. 12:11-12). He will be our advocate before the powers of the world, the powers of darkness.

The Values of Jesus

St. Paul captured for us the values of Jesus Christ in the great Christological hymn of his Letter to the Philippians. He exhorts them:

"Have this mind (i.e. values) among yourselves, which was in Christ Jesus, who, though he was in the form of God, did not count equality with God a thing to be grasped (or a prize to be retained or clung to at all costs), but emptied himself, taking the form of a slave, being born in the likeness of men. And being found in human form he humbled himself and became obedient unto death, even death on a cross. Therefore, God has highly exalted him and bestowed on him the name which is above every name, that at the name of Jesus every knee should bow, in heaven and on earth and under the earth, and every tongue confess that Jesus Christ is Lord, to the glory of God the Father" (Phil. 2:5-11).

So the values of Jesus are: self-emptying, self-surrender, self-gift. In everything that Jesus said or did, in all his life-witness, there was always this manifest trait: nothing but self-emptying, self-surrender, self-gift. Being equal to God, he did not cling to the external trappings of divinity, but emptied himself to take on the form of a slave. Then, being in human form, he humbled or emptied himself further to become obedient, obedient even to death, death on a cross. This last is self-surrender and self-gift, complete surrender and gift of self. Here we have the true theological meaning of 'cross': it does not necessarily entail physical suffering, in some cases it may; but it always and unfailingly means 'gift and surrender of self'. This is the distinguishing trait of Jesus Christ and his Spirit, which is why it is the characteristic quality of anything that is authentically Christian. How spontaneously we say with a certain Christian instinct: if something does not carry the seal or sign of the 'cross', it is not truly Christian! Now we know why: because 'cross' always, unfailingly stands for 'gift and surrender of self'.

This, in fact, is the 'newness' that Jesus Christ brought into our world, the newness of the **New Covenant** or Testament as the Letter to the Hebrews so powerfully inculcates, especially in its chapters 8 and 10. For centuries, the high priests of the Old Covenant had, year after year, on the Day of Atonement, taken the blood of goats and calves and heifers, the blood of animals, to enter the Holy of Holies and offer the sacrifice of atonement, after opening a way through a curtain of canvas. "But when Christ appeared as a high priest of the good things that have come, then through the greater and more perfect tent (not made with hands, that is, not of this creation) he entered once for all into the Holy Place, taking not the blood of goats and calves, **but his own blood**, thus securing an eternal redemption" (Heb. 9:11-12). And "the **new** and living **way** which he opened for us", to enter once and for all into the Holy of Holies was not by the moving aside of a curtain, but, 'through the curtain', that is, through his flesh (Heb. 10:19-20). The same message once again of the gift and surrender of self, not of the blood of animals, is repeated at the beginning of the same Letter, Hebrews chapter 10.

When Christ came into the world, he said, "Sacrifices and offerings thou hast not desired, but a body hast thou prepared for me; in burnt offerings and sin offerings thou hast taken no pleasure. Then I said, 'Lo, I have come to do Thy will, O God, as it is written of me in the scroll of the book'. When he said the above, he abolished the first (covenant) to establish the second. And we have been sanctified through the **offering of the body of Jesus Christ** once for all" (Heb. 10:5-10).

The Risen Jesus

Jesus gives us in all these promises the assurance that the Spirit that he and his Father will send is the Spirit of Truth, the Comforter, the Advocate. Now the Risen Jesus actually fulfilled this promise, the promise we have had in the Last Supper discourse in the Gospel of St. John, chapters 14, 15 and 16. The actual gift of the Spirit was brought by the Risen Jesus when he appeared to his disciples who, for fear of the Jews, had locked themselves behind closed doors. They were all huddled together under one roof, yet there was among them no community. It is not because persons are huddled together under one roof that there is necessarily community. The disciples had lost faith in Jesus – the key to, and secret of, Christian community. They thought everything was over; their world and worldly hopes were shattered by the death of Jesus on the cross. Afraid of the Jews, they locked themselves behind closed doors. And Jesus broke through these closed doors and closed hearts – the Risen Jesus – and said: "Peace be with you". Then he added: "Receive the Holy Spirit". He had earlier promised them the Spirit. Now he gives them that Spirit, the Spirit of peace and reconciliation. For the Risen Jesus continued: "Whose sins you will forgive, they are forgiven them whose sins you retain, they are retained" (cf. Jn. 20:21-23). The Spirit of Peace and Reconciliation!

> ## Know about Jesus final journey to Jerusalem.
> ## Reflect on how the Church celebrates this even on Passion Sunday.

Note: Chief Rabbi Sir Jonathan Sacks reminds the Jews in Britain today of one of the Bible's most brilliant insights. Tell the story, said Moses in the Book of Exodus. When you leave slavery and begin the long journey across the wilderness to freedom, tell the story. When you enter the land, tell the story. In every generation, every year, tell the story. If you want to survive and achieve immortality as a faith, tell the story.

He went further. Don't just recount the story. Relive it, enact it as if it has just happened and was fresh in the memory. Eat matzah, the unleavened bread of affliction, taste maror, the bitter herbs of slavery, and drink four cups of wine, one for each state of liberation."

Consider how you will teach your students the Paschal Mystery this year. How can you make it come **alive** for them so that it will live on in their minds? Think about how you will unfold the events of Holy Week so that your students will want to be in church because now they understand what the services really mean.

Starting Point:
What do you think being a follower of Jesus involves?
What was it like for the disciples?
What does it require of us today?
Can you give examples of what you think Jesus meant when he asked James and John if they could drink the cup that he must drink? (cf. page 70 in the textbook).

Explain that in the next six weeks we are going to journey with Jesus through the most dramatic events of his life on earth. The invitation is for us to enter into a close relationship with him – to be one of his close disciples so that what we study will have a profound impact on our lives.

Jesus' entry into Jerusalem: the day when the cry of the crowds went from cheers to jeers. *(If you have the DVD of Jesus of Nazareth it will help to show the clip of this event).* Take time to meditate on page 71.

Discuss: The crowd shouted 'Hosanna' (Save us now).
What did they want to be saved from?

PPP: Passion Sunday in Church.

Ask students to write a concise 'headline' to summarise what they have learnt in this lesson.

Assessment Folder: Assessment task 'Passion Sunday'.

> **Deepen our understanding of the events of Holy Thursday.**
> **Reflect on the importance of this day for us.**

Starting Point:

Explore the idea of greatness. Imagine a very important person was spending a day in school, what would you expect of them? How do you think they would behave? How would you feel if that person told you not to queue for your lunch but that he would serve you? It was a *little bit* like this for Jesus and the disciples, but much more dramatic and profound.

Jesus transformed our idea of greatness and turned it on its head. The job of washing another person's feet was the task of a low caste slave, the lowest of the low. Jesus took upon himself the role of a servant when he washed the disciples' feet. For Jesus, to be great is not to lord it over others or to seek the higher place, but to serve and lay down his life for us. For us, it means to get out of **self-interest, self-pity** and **self-love** in order to help others.

St. Francis de Sales summed it up by saying that great works do not always lie in our way, but every moment we may do little ones excellently, that is, with great love.

 Audio Recording: The Donkey Owner - Preparation for the Last Supper (for less able students).

 WS 1: The Donkey Owner (for less able students).

 WS 2: Holy Week record of events.

 PPP: The Last Supper Meditation (It is in the folder for Mystery of the Eucharist). This PPP can be used again as a meditation to make a direct link with Holy Thursday.

 PPP: Mass on Holy Thursday.
Use your knowledge about the Jewish celebration of the Passover, what is different and what is the same about this night's celebration?

 Assessment Folder: Choice of three Assessment Tasks.

Know about the Agony in the Garden.
Reflect on how it may help people suffering today.

Starting Point:

Allow time for students to study the pictures of Jesus in the Garden of Gethsemane. Jesus is experiencing incredible agony – yet what does he do? (*Note how Jesus hands over to his Father: "Not my will but thine be done".*) Allow students to ask questions about the problem of suffering.

 PPP: Altar of Repose in church on Holy Thursday.

 WS 3: Gethsemane.

 Audio recording: Trees in the Garden of Gethsemane. Suitable for silent reflection.

Know about the betrayal of Jesus and his trial before the Sanhedrin.
Reflect on situations of betrayal.

Starting Point:

Discuss: What does the word 'betrayal' suggest?

Give an example to illustrate the meaning.

How does it feel to be betrayed?

Think of a situation where you have been let down by someone you trusted. What were your feelings towards that person?

When could it be right to divulge information?

Lead students to understand: when someone else's life is in danger or when a criminal act has been committed.

Draw out that betrayal can be in small matter as well as in serious events – Gestapo – cowardly act of betrayal of Jews and the courageous people who offered them protection.

 Flipchart: Judas.

Explain that the normal greeting of friendship is to kiss on the cheek – to go close to a person means you trust them.

 PPP: Judas.

Background Notes: The temple held a unique place in the religion of the Jews. It was in the temple, in the holy of holies, that God was believed to be present among his Chosen People; it was a sacred place which housed the Ark of the Covenant and was entered by only one man, the High Priest, and that only once a year. So by saying that he was the temple, Jesus was saying that he took over from the temple and it was in him that God was now present among his people. God's presence would no longer be confined to one people but he would be present to everyone who had faith in Christ. See also John 2:19.

 PPP: Trial before the Sanhedrin.

 WS 4: Jesus before the Sanhedrin.

> **Reflect on the trial before Pilate and the Crucifixion.**
> **Make links with the different types of suffering people experience today.**

Starting Point:

The flipchart on Peter's character is best used as a starting point.

 Flipchart: Peter's character.

Role-play:

Work in pairs: one is Peter, the other John.

Peter has always been the natural leader. John is younger than Peter and has always looked up to him. John was very close to Jesus.

What questions would John ask Peter about his recent behaviour?

What would Peter say by way of an explanation?

What self knowledge has Peter gained as a result of recent events?

What previous events in Peter's life might John refer to? (For example: Walking on water Mt. 14:22-23; Jesus washes Peter's feet Jn. 13:2-10).

 Flipchart: Peter and Judas under pressure.

Song: If you have the CD 'Born for This' by CJM, play 'Jesus before Pilate' and 'Pilate's Song'. (To order CD phone 01675 466 254)

 PPP: Trial before Pontius Pilate and background information.

 PPP: and Audio Recording: The Centurion's Monologue. The words of the audio recording are in the 'Other Resources Folder'.

 PPP: Good Friday in Church.

 WS 5: Witnesses.

Other Resources Folder: The Passion (Adapted for three voices).

WS 6: Man to Man – Nicodemus & Pilate.

WS 7: Man to Man – Nicodemus & Pilate (Extension).

WS 8: Peter looks back.

WS 9: Letter to Pilate from the Emperor.

WS 10: Pilate points the finger.

WS 11: Classroom Discussion Statements for activity 5 page 82 of Student's Book.

Assessment Folder: choice of five **Assessment Tasks.**

www.tere.org Go to 'Secondary' click on KS3 Support Material to find 'PeterProgress'.

Understand the meaning of the Resurrection.
Reflect on its importance for us.

Starting Point:

Explain to the students that it is difficult while still in Holy Week to celebrate the Resurrection, nevertheless, it is important to try to help them to experience it as if it has just happened, to relive, give the the opportunity to role-play the events.

 **PPP: Easter Vigil in Church.**

Song: If you have the CD 'Born for This', play numbers 31 and 32: 'The Resurrection' and 'We thought that it was over'. CJM Music www.cjmmusic.com

Flipchart: Mary of Magdala.

NB Make sure there is time for students to do the activities on page 87.
Allow time for students to make connections and perceive the relevance of the Resurrection of Jesus for their own lives.

www.tere.org Go to 'Secondary' click on KS3 Support Material to find 'Court Resurrection':
Imagine you are one of the disciples called up to answer charges.

Assessment Folder: choice of two **Assessment Tasks.**

Jesus before the Sanhedrin

1. Read Matthew 26: 57-68 and answer the following questions:
   a) When Jesus was arrested where was he taken?
   b) Who was present at the trial?
   c) Who followed Jesus and the guards to the courtyard?
   d) What was the first question Jesus was asked?
   e) What reply did Jesus give?
   f) What evidence did they find against Jesus so that they could put him to death?
   g) Why were the chief priest and elders so determined to put Jesus to death?
   h) What sentence did Jesus get?
   i) Was the trial a just one? Give reasons for your answer.

2. Explain the following words using the phrases in the box below:
   The Christ   **Sanhedrin**   **Blasphemy**   **High Priest**

   > The Jewish high court of law.
   > The Messiah, meaning 'the anointed one', chosen by God.
   > Caiaphas, he was the head of the Sanhedrin.
   > This is to act, or say something that would offend God.

3. Imagine you are Peter, outline the part you played in accompanying your Lord and Master since you left the Last Supper table and how you are feeling now.

Man to Man – Let us Talk Nicodemus and Pilate.

Complete the speech bubbles for Pilate.

1. Last Friday, I watched as your soldiers brought the Nazarene to you. What did you do?

2. Your soldiers mocked this man and you looked on. What were you thinking?

3. You washed your hands of him. Why?

4. You handed him over to be crucified! Why? What did you hope to achieve?

5. By now, you must have heard the recent report about this Nazarene? Where does that leave you?

For Extended Talk see WS 10 on DVD ROM

Peter

Activities

1. Use speech boxes to express what you think were the most intense thoughts and feelings Peter experienced during these events.

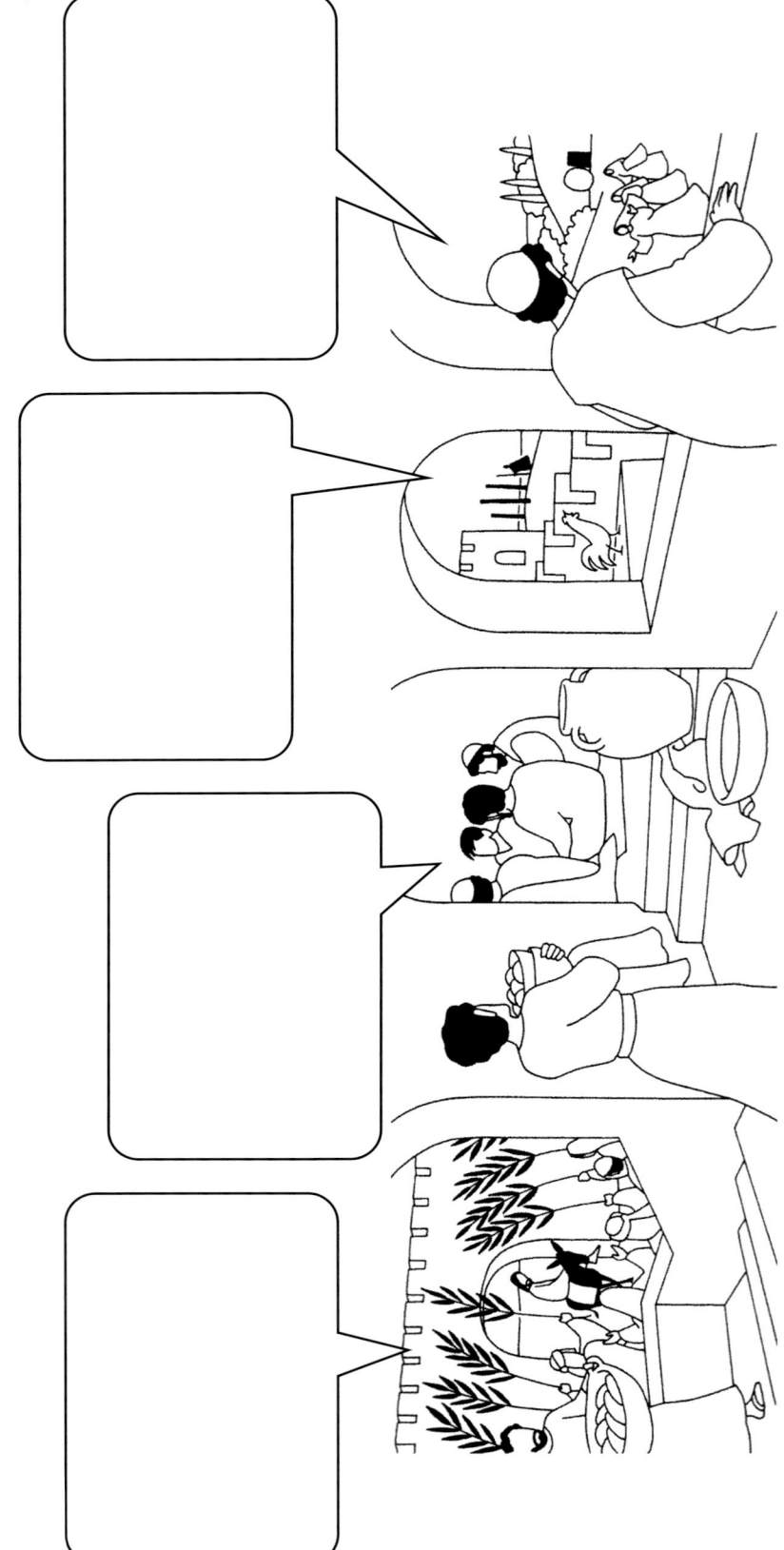

2. Peter is a good example for all Christians to follow. Do you agree? Give reasons for your answer showing that you have considered more than one point of view.

FROM TIBERIUS JULIUS CAESAR AUGUSTUS, EMPEROR OF ROME, TO PROCURATOR PONTIUS PILATE IN THE PROVINCE OF JUDEA:

Greetings,

Reports have reached me here in Rome of a near-riot in Jerusalem during the religious festival of the Jewish people known as Passover. I understand that it was all started when a certain Nazarene was presented to you for judgement by the Sanhedrin - the Jewish authorities. Is this true? Who was this man? Was he a terrorist, an anarchist, a genuine threat to Rome or not?

I have also been informed that you handed him over for ritualistic humiliation - allowing our soldiers to mock him as a king. Why did you allow this?

I have asked my contacts in Judea to compile a dossier on this man. Their findings indicate that for the past two to three years he has been a force for good, rather than a threat to our Empire. They say that he has been going round healing the sick, consoling the downtrodden, preaching a message of love and tolerance, feeding the hungry and even bringing dead people back to life! Were these the actions of a man who deserved death at the hands of Roman authority? How do you justify your actions, Procurator?

I've even heard that this man said it was right to pay taxes to Caesar - which, of course, it is! So what was your problem with him?

And now, perhaps most worryingly, I hear that his followers are claiming that he is alive again - even though all the reports state categorically that he died by crucifixion on Calvary. Even your own Centurion confirms that.

So what are you proposing to do about this new sect that is emerging in Jerusalem among those who believe the Nazarene has been resurrected?
I await your response with interest and anticipation, and would remind you that within the next few months I shall be considering who to appoint where in the Empire, and no one is secure in his post.

DICTATED IN THE IMPERIAL PALACE IN ROME AND SIGNED BY TIBERIUS JULIUS CAESAR AUGUSTUS, IMPERATOR, 1 JUNE IN THE 19TH YEAR OF HIS IMPERIAL REIGN.

Task

Imagine you are Pilate. Write a reply to the Emperor.
- Answer each of his questions.
- Explain how you feel about the situation now.
- Suggest what you think you ought to do and why.

8.5 The Mission of the Church

Religious Education Curriculum Directory

"The Church's Mission is that of Christ its Head. The ultimate purpose of this mission is to enable all people to share in the communion of life and love of the Father, Son and Holy Spirit. To this end the Church is called to express in society the mission of Christ as priest, prophet and king, calling every person to the worship of God alone, advocating the cause of the poorest and witnessing to the right order of society." (p. 19).

Attainment Target 1: Learning *about* the Catholic faith.
Attainment Target 2: Learning *from* the Catholic faith.

Key Learning Objectives:
- Deepen our understanding of the Church.
  o Reflect on what it means for us.

- Understand the Mission of the Church.
  o Reflect on what it involves.

- Understand the importance of living-out the teaching of Jesus.
  o Reflect on the work of the SVP.

- Know about some people who have dedicated their lives to helping the homeless.
  o Reflect on what we can learn from them.

- Understand the importance of helping people with disabilities.
  o Reflect on how they can help us.

- Understand how the Taizé Community helps young people from all over the world to live the Gospel.
  o Reflect on why it is a powerful experience for them.

- Be aware of the challenges to the mission of the Church.
  o Reflect on the help young people give.

Theological Notes

The Church as "People of God"

Chapter two of **Lumen Gentium** is devoted to the image of the Church as the 'People of God'.

What are the theological and spiritual depths of this 'People of God' image of the Church? The 'People of God' is first of all not some altogether new beginning. It is in clear continuity with the People of God with whom God made the covenant on Mt. Sinai: our roots are in the Old Testament, in that people whom God chose and with whom he made his covenant, constituting them as *his own people* (cf. Ex. 19:3-6; 24:1-8). And yet, this 'People of God', which is the Church of Jesus Christ, is a *new* People of God; on this *newness* we shall dwell a little later. Further, this 'People of God' is 'on the move': it is a *pilgrim people*, marching through history, *real* human history – **not** some airy-fairy, dream-world entity – marching forward to the completion and consummation of its mystery as 'People of God'. It is quite moving to read in Chapter two of **Lumen Gentium,** the various stages which God in his love prepared from all eternity, of his plan and design for our salvation – the stages of this 'mystery of the Church'. God first **prefigured** this 'mystery' in creation; then, in a second phase of **preparation**, he prepared 'the Church' with the Old Testament 'People of God'; later came Jesus Christ who, through some special deeds **actuated** or made actual the setting-up or institution of the **new** 'People of God' in clear continuity with the old 'People of God'. Still later, we have the **public manifestation** or revelation of this 'People of God' on the day of Pentecost with the outpouring of the Holy Spirit, when the Church, the new 'People of God', was born publicly. This new people, now publicly manifested, begins its ongoing march through history which has not yet finished, because it is moving, says **Lumen Gentium,** towards its **consummation** at the end of time; this will be at the Second Coming of the Lord, when he will come to gather his people and take them on to the fulfilment of the Kingdom.

At this juncture, we need to spell out two important consequences of what we have just exposed of the Church as 'People of God'. The first is that of facing a very real risk of a distorted modern-day analysis and interpretation of the Church as 'People of God'. Not a few of our contemporaries approach this biblical reality with a sociological understanding of the term 'people'. Having culled from studies on human society what a 'people' is, some of our contemporaries wish to add on to this sociological reality its specifying element: it is not just any 'people', but the 'People of God'. This kind of approach is fraught with serious risks: for it starts with 'people' as a sociological reality, to which is added the fact that God enters into this reality, because God chooses it and makes it his own. And so, we have Christians and Catholics today who are spearheading movements, so-called movements of renewal, based on a heavily-accentuated sociological understanding of the mystery of the Church. The fact is that the starting-point is **not** a 'people' in the sociological sense; the take-off point is **not** sociological at all. It is **God** who takes the initiative in intervening to set up this group of scattered tribes as a 'people' – indeed, **his own people** – by making a covenant with it. Under the saving initiative and primacy of God's love, Moses had got together and led these scattered tribes out of Egypt. The specifying element is clearly, then, *God's initiative of love* and *God's covenant* – **God**, who constitutes those scattered tribes as a people, as *his own* people. Thus it is God who says, "You were no people, now you will be a people, my people, and I will be your God".

In what exactly does this **newness** of this *new* 'People of God' consist? We have insisted on the *continuity* of this *new* 'People of God' with the Old Testament 'People of God'. If, then, there is **newness** in the New Testament 'People of God', there is also a certain specific *discontinuity* with the Old Testament 'People of God'. What is this *discontinuity* which makes of the New Testament 'People of God' a *new*

'People of God'? The answer lies in the **covenant** made by God. God's covenant made at Mt. Sinai was the specifying element that constituted the group of scattered tribes into a 'people', God's chosen people, *God's own* people. Now, we know that there is a new covenant which God made in and through his Son Jesus Christ; we must underscore, however, how God made this *new* covenant, and in what exactly lies its **newness**. Jesus Christ did **not** make it in the blood of a lamb or of any animal; he made it in **his own blood**. This is the whole burden of the Letter to the Hebrews in sharply contrasting the New Testament priesthood of Jesus Christ with the priesthood of the Old Testament. Jesus Christ is the unique and *only* priest of the New Testament, in whom alone all other New Testament priests are priests. Whereas the sacrifices offered by the Old Testament priests were sacrifices made in the blood of animals (bulls, goats, calves or lambs) – that is, the offering of something outside of, external to, the priest offering the sacrifice – Jesus Christ did not offer something outside of himself: he shed **his own blood**, he **handed over himself**. So the Old Testament covenant on Mt. Sinai was made in the blood of an animal (cf. Ex. 24:3-8); the New Testament covenant was made in Jesus Christ's own blood (cf. Mt. 26:27-28; Mk. 14:23-24; Lk. 22:20; 1 Cor. 11:25). The Letter to the Hebrews underlines the same very strongly in Chapters 9 and 10 (Heb. 9:12; 15.18-20, 24-26; 10:4-10, 19-20). Jesus did not enter into the Holy of Holies once a year, as did the High Priests of the Old Testament with the blood of an animal. Jesus did not pull aside a curtain of canvas to enter the Holy of Holies. He broke open a **new** way through his own flesh, and entered once and for all into the Holy of Holies with **his own blood – himself**. In all of **this** lies the **newness** of the *new* 'People of God'. If we have not grasped **this newness** of the **handing over of ourselves** (**not** of something outside of ourselves), we have not understood at all the depths of the mystery of the Church as the 'People of God'.

We can, therefore, best close our exposition of the mystery of the Church as 'People of God' by citing a very pertinent text from the First Letter of St. Peter: 1 Pet. 2. This is one of the richest synthesis texts of the whole New Testament. Among its first verses we read these significant words: "Come to him (namely, to Jesus Christ), to that living stone rejected by men, but in God's sight chosen and precious; and you, like living stones, be yourselves built into a spiritual house, to be a holy priesthood, to offer spiritual sacrifices acceptable to God through Jesus Christ" (1 Pet. 2:4-5). So, not only is Jesus Christ priest, temple and sacrifice, but every single Christian is, in and with Jesus Christ, priest and temple and sacrifice. In this precise context it is that St. Peter gives us, in verses 9 and 10, the rich biblical backdrop to contemplating that mystery of the Church as the 'People of God': "You, then, are a chosen race, a royal priesthood, a holy nation, God's own people, that you may declare the wonderful deeds of him who called you out of darkness into his marvellous light. Once you were no people, but now you are God's people ..." (1 Pet. 2:9-10). In these words we recognise the *continuity* of the New Testament People of God with that people constituted by God at Mt. Sinai when he made a covenant with them, for we read in the Book of Exodus: "You have seen what I did to the Egyptians, and how I bore you on eagles' wings and brought you to myself. Now, therefore, if you will obey my voice and keep my covenant, you shall be my own possession among all peoples; for all the earth is mine, and you shall be to me a kingdom of priests and a holy nation" (Ex. 19:4-6). But in the passage we have cited from 1 Pet. 2:4-5, we are also given the *distinctive newness* of the New Testament 'People of God' for, in Jesus

Christ, priest, temple and sacrifice, every single baptised Christian is priest, temple and sacrifice, offering **spiritual** sacrifices acceptable to God through Jesus Christ. These 'spiritual' sacrifices (namely, sacrifices vivified and animated by the Spirit of Jesus Christ) have as their essence what is characteristic of the unique New Testament priest and priesthood – that is, the *handing over of self in love*, not the sacrifices which offered the blood of animals. Doubtless, all of this only confirms us in recognising in the Church as the 'People of God' that divine, transcendent, salvific reality revealed and manifested in visible and even human form, which is the deep biblical understanding of 'mystery'.

The Church as "Body of Christ"

It is St. Paul who, over and over again in his letters, uses this image to speak of the mystery of the Church. However, he uses the image in two distinct ways: one in his so-called 'Greater Letters', of which we shall consider two (*Romans* and *1 Corinthians*); and the other in his 'Captivity Letters' or letters from prison, like the Letters to the *Ephesians* and to the *Colossians*. In *Romans* and *1 Corinthians* Paul speaks of the 'Body of Christ' as applied to *the local Church*: the whole local Church in Rome or in Corinth is the 'Body of Christ'. In the 'Captivity Letters', however, he employs the image of the 'Body of Christ' **not** as applied to the local Church: it is *the universal Church* which is the 'Body of Christ', and Christ is the Head of the Body. So then, in the case of the 'Captivity Letters', the 'Body of Christ', which is the universal Church, is like the body's trunk, for Christ is the Head of this Body.

1. *The "Greater Letters": Romans and 1 Corinthians*

In Rom. 12 and 1 Cor. 12, Paul speaks of the Church as the 'Body of Christ'. We shall take, somewhat in detail, *1 Cor. 12*. This passage can only be understood and interpreted in the context of the division prevailing in the local Church of Corinth. Everybody was claiming charisms, everybody was claiming special gifts of the Spirit. Dealing with this situation, St. Paul admits that the Spirit does give these gifts differently to different persons according to the measure of the Spirit's giving, his liberality, his freedom in giving. There are many gifts, varieties of gifts, but there is **one** Spirit. There are many members, but there is only **one** Body, vivified by **one** Spirit (cf. 1 Cor. 12: 4-13). The sum and substance of Paul's teaching here, in the context of the very real division existing in the local Church of Corinth, is that, just as the human body has different members each of which has a different function while the body remains *one single body*, so in the Body of Christ, which is the Church, there are many gifts given freely by the Spirit, but the Spirit is **one**, and the Church, which is the Body of Christ, is **one**.

In the same context, Paul moves on to suggest that while there are such charisms or gifts which are certainly genuine, perhaps some of the gifts being claimed by some individuals may well not be genuine and authentic. Hence such gifts need to be tested or 'discerned'; this test is **love** – **genuine**

love (cf. 1 Cor. 12:27-13:3). Knowing already in his time, as we very well do especially today, that 'love' is one of the cheapest words to be bandied about, Paul feels constrained to spell out, from his contemplation of God's way and kind of loving, the qualities of genuine love. Though he enumerates no less than sixteen of these qualities, we realise that he is only offering various expressions of one central quality which he emphasises almost half-way through his list: **"Love does not seek its own interest"** (1 Cor. 13:5). Is this not the characteristic acid-test and touchstone of authentic love? True and genuine love forgets itself, renounces self, gives and surrenders self – in a word, **hands itself over** – that **newness** of the New Testament of which we have spoken earlier.

2. *The 'Captivity Letters': Ephesians and Colossians*

Here, too, it will help us to dwell for a while on **Ephesians 4**. We note that this passage is once again written in the context of promoting 'union' and 'unity': "I, therefore, a prisoner for the Lord, beg you to lead a life worthy of the calling to which you have been called, with all lowliness and meekness, with patience, forbearing one another in love, eager to maintain the unity of the Spirit in the bond of peace. There is one body and one Spirit, just as you were called to one hope that belongs to your call, one Lord, one faith, one baptism, one God and Father of us all, who is above all and through all and in all. But grace is given to each of us according to the measure of Christ's gift" (Eph. 4:1-7).

In the context of such an appeal for 'union' and 'unity', then, Paul comes to speak of the 'Body of Christ': "And his gifts were that some should be apostles, some prophets, some evangelists, some pastors and teachers, in roles of service to help make the faithful ready to build up the Body of Christ, till we become one in faith and in the knowledge of God's Son and reach mature personhood in Christ. All this, in such a way that we may no longer be children tossed here and there by every wind of doctrine that originates in human trickery and skill in proposing error. Rather, living and speaking the truth in love, we are to grow up in every way into him who is the Head, into Christ; from him the whole Body grows and, with the proper functioning of the members joined firmly together by each supporting ligament, builds itself up in love" (Eph. 4:11-16).

One immediate reflection on our part, at this stage, is to ask ourselves whether this Pauline image of the mystery of the Church as the 'Body of Christ' adds anything to its earlier image as 'People of God'. We realise that the 'People of God' image, by itself, indicates no particularly intimate life-union between God or Christ on the one hand and the Church on the other. But the image of the 'Body of Christ' speaks eloquently of the intimate union between Christ (the Head) and the Church (his Body) – such intimate union, in fact, that Christ, as Head, becomes the life-giving, vivifying principle of the Body, the principle that makes life flow into the Body: there is such intimate organic unity between the Head and the members that the Head becomes the living life-principle building up the Body. This is manifest not only in Eph. 4:11-16 which we have cited above; it is once again in evidence in Col. 2:17-19 (where verse 19 is almost a word-for-word repetition of Eph. 4:16**)**.

It is interesting to note that Paul attributes to Christ as Head the quality of 'governing principle' in the sense of 'sovereign power, authority and dominion', as we read explicitly in Eph. 1:20-23 (especially in verse 23). These aspects of 'governing principle' and 'organic life-giving principle' attributed to Christ as Head are not to be seen as disparate or disjunctive aspects; they are to be synthesised and integrated, as Paul himself makes clear in his marvellous Christological hymn of cosmic sweeping dimensions in his Letter to the Colossians (Col. 1:12-20). In it Paul proclaims that everything that has been created *in* Christ Jesus, *through* Christ Jesus, *for* Christ Jesus. In other words, Christ Jesus is the **Alpha** and the **Omega** of all creation and all re-creation: Not only, "in him all things were created in heaven and on earth …, *whether thrones or dominions or principalities or authorities*" (Col. 1:16) – that is, he is the 'governing principle', but also, "he is the Head of his Body, the Church; the beginning, the first-born from the dead … in him all the fullness of God was pleased to dwell" (Col. 1:18-19 – that is, the Risen One who is the fullness of life and the source of life: he is the 'living and life-giving principle'). **And all this**, "reconciling all things … making peace **by the blood of his cross**" (Col. 1:20), echoing what is said in Eph. 1:13-16: "in Christ Jesus you who once were far off have been brought near **in the blood of Christ** … so making peace and **reconciling us to God in one Body through the Cross**" – to paraphrase it equivalently, **all this, by handing himself over in love**.

Jesus' Mission

Jesus begins his active apostolic mission after his baptism and temptations in the desert.

"And Jesus returned in the power of the Spirit into Galilee … and he taught in (the) synagogues, being glorified by all. And he came to Nazareth, where he had been brought up; and he went to the synagogue, as his custom was, on the Sabbath day. And he stood up to read; and there was given to him the book of the prophet Isaiah: He opened the book and found the place where it was written, 'The Spirit of the Lord is upon me, because he has anointed me to preach good news to the poor. He has sent me to proclaim release to the captives and recovering of sight to the blind, to set at liberty those who are oppressed, to proclaim the acceptable year of the Lord.' And he closed the book, and gave it back to the attendant and sat down; and the eyes of all in the synagogue were fixed on him. And he began to say to them, 'Today, this scripture has been fulfilled in your hearing'" (Lk. 4:14-21).

It is highly significant that Jesus, at the very start of his active apostolic ministry cites Is. 61 on the Spirit anointing him to preach the Gospel to the poor, the gospel of release and freedom for those held captive, and to set at liberty those who are down-trodden and oppressed. Jesus himself proclaiming his Spirit as Spirit of freedom: not only freeing him **from** the wiles, snares and attacks of the evil spirit in the temptations, but all this as a preparation to be **'free for'** his whole-hearted service to the poor, making him a channel and instrument to free all those in bondage, all those oppressed and in need of liberation and freedom.

We think of Mother Teresa, a woman filled with the Spirit of God. Opening her heart to God's Spirit early in life, she allowed him to lead her. Filled with his love, God's personal love who is the Spirit of God, she was driven by that same love to dedicate her entire life and all her energies to freeing the poorest of the poor.

The Spirit of God in our lives

The Spirit of God frees us, but only to make us, out of love, instruments of freedom for others. Only such an outreach of being channels and instruments of the Spirit's liberating action, especially for those of our brothers and sisters who are oppressed and downtrodden, is a guarantee that we are indeed led by the Spirit of the Lord. There are, of course, many ways of being 'downtrodden and oppressed', not just material poverty, though we are intensely aware of the dire need of the vast masses of such poor people in our land. Yet all around us stalks every sort of misery and poverty, not the least of which is spiritual misery and poverty. Hundreds, thousands are hungering for God. If we relieve the materially poor of their bodily and material misery and poverty, it is to be able to satisfy their deeper thirst and their more intense hunger – their hunger and thirst for God. Were we just to stop at relieving their material poverty, we would not really be building up the Kingdom of God. Of course, we **have to** give them bread to eat, if they are hungry (cf. for example, Jn. 6:1-14): but after Jesus had done so, he did not fail to direct the hearts of the same crowds beyond and above their mere "eating their fill of the loaves": "Do not labour for the food which perishes", he warned, "but for the food, which endures to eternal life, which the Son of Man will give to you; for on him has God the Father set his seal" (Jn. 6:26-27).

People are hungering, thirsting for God particularly in our land, which down the centuries has been marked by this intense 'quest for God'. As we walk down our crowded streets, people walking alongside us are hungering and thirsting for Christ Jesus even if they are not consciously aware of it. Christ Jesus is, in fact, for every man and woman 'life' and 'light', "the way, the truth and the life", indeed, their unique Saviour. If we ourselves are not filled with the Spirit of Christ Jesus, we cannot be channels and instruments of his freeing action for these our brothers and sisters. The searching question we need to ask ourselves, if indeed we are not channels of freedom for others, is whether we are **truly free** ourselves at any rate, whether we are persevering in giving God and his Spirit 'a real chance' in our day-to-day living.

Deepen our understanding of the Church.
Reflect on what it means for us.

Starting Point:

Try to have newspaper cuttings and details of incidents where Christianity is being challenged or undermined today. Invite the students to share how they feel their faith is being challenged. How can they support and encourage one another? What is likely to happen if we do not have the courage to openly profess our faith? Encourage students to think deeply about their faith.

 ### Flipchart: Challenges to Christianity.

Images of the Church:

You may wish to start off with: Think – Pair – Share.
What or who do you think the Church is? Students think on their own and write down their response; then, they tell the person next to them in order to generate more ideas and after that share their thinking with the whole class.

 ### Flipchart: Body of Christ.

Help students to understand that Jesus as Head of the Body becomes life-giving to the Body. It is Jesus who makes life flow into the Body of People and builds up the Body. In Jesus "all the fullness of God was pleased to dwell and through him to reconcile to himself all things, whether on earth or in heaven, making peace by the blood of the cross" (Col. 1:19-20). All this has happened by Jesus handing himself over in love for us.

 ### Flipchart: Church as a Community.

It is only when we understand that we are the Church, we are the ones who are being called to respond to the invitation to let Jesus into our lives so that he can transform us by his love. It is Jesus who will help us to think of the needs of others, not just material needs but if we live united to Jesus, he will give us the courage and conviction to share our faith and belief in him.

 ### Pause to Reflect:

"Past the seeker on the prayer rug, came the cripple and the beggar and the beaten. And seeing them, the Holy One went down, down into deep prayer and cried, 'Great God! How is it that a loving Creator can see such things and yet do nothing about them?' And out of the long, long silence, God said, 'I did do something about them. I made you'."
(J. Chittister, *Winds of Change*, p. 144).

Reflect:

Blessed are those who are willing to let go of selfishness and self-centeredness,
for they will become a healing presence.
Blessed are those who are willing to listen with compassion,
for they will become compassionate.

The following Power Point presentations will help to reinforce and summarise the content in the Student's Book.

 PPP: The People of God.

 PPP: The Body of Christ.

 PPP: The Community.

 Assessment Folder: "There's probably no God. Now, stop worrying and enjoy our life".

> **Understand the Mission of the Church.**
> **Reflect on what it involves.**

Starting Point:

Invite students to share what they think is the mission of the Church and then relate it to who **IS** the Church.

Explain that God **sees – hears – is conscious of** human misery and suffering. Our God is neither blind nor deaf nor unaffected by what people have to go through. He always sides with those who are in need, the lonely and those who are denied their basic rights.

However, the puzzle starts here. If God is concerned why doesn't he do something about it? God chooses people as his representatives to do the work **for Him**. God has a plan for each one of us. *(You may wish to recall how God was with Moses all through his life and eventually how God used him to liberate the slaves in Egypt.)*

 Flipcharts: Living the Mission.

Note: we may not be called to do great things but we are all called to do little things with love. St. Thérèse of Lisieux understood that her mission was to love. She decided to be kindest to the people she liked least, to give them a smile and if she could, do some little thing to help them.

WS 1: Mission of St. Thérèse of Lisieux.

 PPP: Mission of St. Thérèse in Britain.

The sceptics looked on in amazement as coach loads of people arrived from all over Great Britain. For the people, it was not superstition, there was no magic, no visible miracles but the relics were a sign that the simple goodness of the saint is open to everyone.

 PPP: A Missionary Sister in the Philippines.

 Assessment Folder: Assessment tasks.

Plenary - Think & Share; list three things the person next to you has learnt today.

> **Understand the importance of living out the teaching of Jesus.**
> **Reflect on the work of the SVP.**

Starting Point:

You may wish to start with a reflection:

When Jesus was on earth, he was determined to reveal God as the one who is understanding, forgiving and loving.

 This is the God who says to each one of us:
I am there – when you are alone.
I am there – when someone hurts you.
I am there – when your world falls apart.
I am there – when you have a bad conscience.
I am there – when others reject you.
I am there – when you are anxious and afraid.
I am there – like an angel who protects you in great need.
I am there – when you call on me.

Think of a time when you were worried, alone, frightened or in great need. Who was it that came to help you? God does work through other people.

 PPP: The Passage – Centre for the homeless in London.

WS 2: The Passage – an account of life in 'The Passage' by Mike Clarke, Chief Executive.

Plenary:

List all the things that take place in your school to help those in need.

Which aspects of the teaching of Jesus best fit:

- The SVP;
- The Passage;
- Your school.

Explain why it is important to live-out the teaching of Jesus.

 PPP: The Columban Sisters.

Imagine you have been appointed by the Vatican to evaluate the life and work of the Columban Sisters in Lima, Peru to see how they are living-out the Mission of the Church.

a) Read pages 90-91 in your textbook on the Church.

b) Make a check list of the key points you will want to examine.

c) In pairs, check to see if your have all the key points on the Church as:

- the People of God;
- the Body of Jesus Christ;
- a Community.

d) Now watch the Power Point Presentation of the Columban Sisters.

e) Watch the presentation again and tick your checklist.

f) In pairs, check your findings.

g) Write your own report for the Vatican.

Note: The Saint Vincent de Paul Society includes 875,000 members in 47,000 Conferences (teams) in 131 countries on five continents.

> **Know about some people who have dedicated their lives to helping the homeless.**
> **Reflect on what we can learn from them.**

Starting Point:

In Britain, not many people will have heard of the life of St. Alberto Hurtado but you have only to put his name into Google to find out about the devotion to him in South America.

Ask the students to be ready to give a summary at the end of the lesson of the reasons why they think he is so well known in Chile and the chief reasons for his canonization.

 PPP: Alberto Hurtado.

Flipcharts: Alberto Hurtado.

 WS 3: Guided activity: "We should not give money to the homeless in the streets because that only encourages them to be lazy." Discuss.

 WS 4: Dorothy Day – A radical devotion.

 Audio Recording: Dorothy Day.

 Assessment Folder: Assessment Task on Alberto Hurtado.

 Flipchart: L'Arche.

> ### Understand that the Taizé Community helps young people from over the world to live the Gospel.
> ### Reflect on why it is a powerful experience for them.

Starting Point:

In preparation for this lesson ask students to watch the evening news and on a sheet of paper make three columns a) 'Good News', b) 'Bad News', c) 'Causes'.

Take time to recapitulate on the wonderful people you studied in the module: SVP groups, Sr. Paula, Columban Sisters, all the volunteers in the Passage, Jean Vanier, Fr. William, St. Alberto Hurtado and those who carry on his work today. In a humble way, all these people are the co-workers of Jesus Christ:

"Christ has no body now on earth but yours. Yours are the only hands with which he can do his work… Yours are the only eyes through which his compassion can shine upon a troubled world. Christ has no body now on earth but yours." St. Teresa of Avila

Another example is Brother Roger, an extraordinary person who has drawn millions of young people into close communion with Jesus.

Videos of Taizé on DVD ROM: there are two videos, one lasting nine minutes and the other fifteen.

 PPP: Taizé.

 **Assessment Folder:** Two assessment tasks on Taizé.

> **Be aware of the challenges to the mission of the Church.**
> **Reflect on the help young people give today.**

Starting Point:

Create an atmosphere of stillness, light some candles and slowly read aloud the parable of the Sower (Lk. 8:4-10)

Read again the answer Jesus gave when the disciples asked what it might mean. Allow the students to make suggestions. Then read (Lk. 8:11-15) and allow time for reflection before doing the activity in the textbook.

 WS 5: Pauline Jaricot – What one girl could do!

 WS 6: Mother Teresa.

 Audio Recording: Mother Teresa and her community.

WS 7: The Mission of Forgiveness, Archbishop Vincent Nichols.
Read 'A Life that Matters' page 12 'The Truth'.

www.tere.org Go to 'Secondary' click on KS3 Support Material to find '1 Cor. 12'. "There is a variety of gifts but always the same Spirit …."

 Assessment Folder: Three assessment tasks.

The following Power Point presentations should be used towards the end of this module to recap. on the most important aspects of it.

 PPPs: The Church as People of God
The Church as Body of Christ
The Church as Community.

PRAYER

Lord make me an instrument of Your peace:
   where there is hatred, let me sow love;
   where there is injury, let me sow pardon;
   where there is doubt, let me sow faith;
   where there is despair, let me give hope;
   where there is darkness, let me give light;
   where there is sadness, let me give joy.

St. Francis of Assisi

Activities

1. Study the images of the Church on pages 90–91 of 'The Truth'.
   a) Which image of the Church best fits the work of the SVP?
   b) Write the name of the image in the SVP box below and give at least three reasons for your choice.

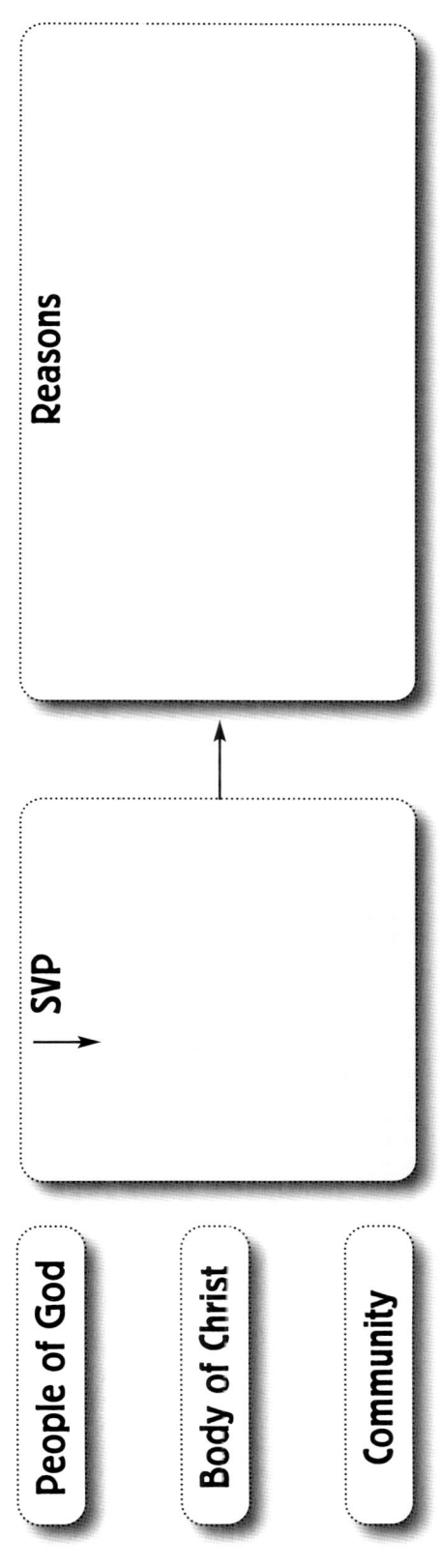

People of God

Body of Christ

Community

SVP

Reasons

2. a) What do you think are the religious beliefs and teachings that inspire and motivate the members of the St. Vincent de Paul Society?
   b) How do your religious beliefs inspire your actions?

Dorothy Day

At the age of 14, Dorothy Day walked around the streets of West Chicago in the USA and witnessed at first hand the conditions in which people were living. Their homes were slums; they had little food or clothing. At first, she became angry and thought of helping them through political action.

Later, Dorothy believed that God wanted her to help these people in a different way. She didn't know how, but she prayed about it and was utterly convinced that:

"The mystery of the poor is this: that they are Jesus, and what you do for them you do for him. It is the only way we have of knowing and believing in our love. The mystery of poverty is that by sharing in it, making ourselves poor in giving to others, we increase our knowledge of and belief in love". (From Selected Writings)

Dorothy was convinced of God's continuing promise to us that He is with us always, with His comforts and joy, if only we will ask. Her Catholic faith led her and others to open Houses of Hospitality across America where poor people could come for meals, clothes and accommodation. She also campaigned for improved rights for workers, and helped start the Catholic Worker Movement.

Activity

1. Why do you think Dorothy became angry when she saw the slums in West Chicago?

2. How might she have helped them through political action?

3. By helping the poor Dorothy helped herself as well. Explain with reference to the teaching of Jesus and your own experience of helping others.

4. a) Read about Dorothy's work and her experiences.
      (DVD ROM Dorothy Day – A Radical Devotion)
   b) Show how she fulfilled the mission of the Church.

Pauline Jaricot (1789-1862)

What one girl could do!

Pauline Jaricot was born in France in 1789. When she was sixteen, she decided to spend her life serving God. She was searching for a way to help the missions so that all people would come to know Jesus Christ and the Gospel.

Eventually, she had a plan which she shared with her close friends and asked for their support. This was to pray daily for the missions and to contribute one cent a week to support them. Each friend agreed to find ten others who would do the same. In a very short time, tens became hundreds and hundreds became thousands. By 1821, it had 2000 members. The offerings were all sent to one central treasurer.

In 1822, this project was taken over by the Vatican. It became the official missionary organisation for the whole Church. It is known as the **Society for the Propagation of the Faith**. To this day, money is still collected in all the churches for the missions.

By 1826, Pauline had another plan. She started the Association of the **'Living Rosary'**. The fifteen decades of the Rosary were divided among fifteen friends. They agreed that each day, they would recite one decade (one 'Our Father', ten 'Hail Mary's' and one 'Glory be to the Father' while thinking of one particular mystery of the Rosary). Ten years later, more than one million people had joined the **'Living Rosary'**.

Activity

1. In small groups discuss:
   a) If Pauline was alive today, what do you think she would consider as the greatest spiritual need in the United Kingdom? Try to give specific examples.
   b) Why do you think these needs exist?
   c) What do you think could be done meet these needs?

2. a) Share your ideas with the rest of the class.
   b) Is there anything as a class or a group that you can do to take your ideas forward?

3. Research on the Internet 'Society of the Propagation of the Faith'. Summarize its main work and achievements.

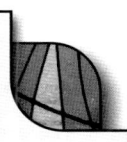

The Power of Forgiveness

Archbishop Vincent Nichols

To forgive is very difficult and costly.

Thinking about forgiveness is not that easy, yet every time I read the newspapers or watch television we hear about people who do wrong and cause suffering to others. And then people always talk about **getting even** with each other, getting their own back.

Now, you know that is quite understandable because **to forgive somebody is very difficult and costly.** If you or I are going to ask to be forgiven for what we have done then we really have to start by looking closely at the damage that we have done to cause people to suffer. So we have to start by taking our own actions seriously and decide to change - to behave differently in the future.

1. a) Write down the key points of the above paragraph?
   b) What is the most important point to remember?

Forgiveness means changing our mind and our heart.
If we are asked to forgive somebody who has hurt us that is difficult as well, because that means that we have to let go of our hurt, to say, "All right, I will put that behind me".
It means changing our mind and our heart - it means setting off on a whole new path.

   c) What do we need to keep in mind when we ask for forgiveness?

What does Jesus teach us?

Now, Jesus teaches us what is true. He even asks us to forgive our enemies. He said: "Do good to those who hate you and pray for those who persecute you".

Think of what Jesus did. When he was being crucified on the cross, he asked his Father to forgive those who were crucifying him. He said: "Father forgive them, because they do not know what they are doing". He made excuses for those who were driving the nails into his own hands.

So Jesus is the one who refuses to retaliate, he is not interested in getting even, even though it means he dies. Now in our Christian faith, following Jesus, we believe forgiveness is a gift of God. It is not something that we can do of ourselves.

Certainly we have to understand ourselves as deeply as we can, we have to be willing to face what we have done, we have to be generous even towards ourselves, but in the end we believe that if we are to forgive another person, God has got to be working in us.

> **d) What example does Jesus give us?**

What do we need most of all?

We need the grace of God. It is God's power in our minds and hearts that we need in order to take that extra step and truly forgive another person.

There is a little bit of scripture that I think not many people read. You could if you look at chapter 16 in the Gospel of St. John. There is a little phrase and it says this: "The Holy Spirit will convince the world of sin". Now I think that means that it is only when God gives us light in our minds and a new attitude in our hearts do we really understand the true meaning of sin; the real importance of what we have done wrong; the real impact of the hurt that we have caused. So what we believe, and what you are studying is true, it is only under the influence of the Holy Spirit, only with God within us, that we can truly forgive and make this world new.

> **e) How do you think we can get this grace?**

2. **What do you think is the Power of Forgiveness?**
   Think about:
   - How do you feel when you have hurt someone?
   - What it is like when that person truly forgives you?
   - When someone has really hurt you and you take the step to forgive that person – how does that make you feel?
   - When members of a family or group are ready to forgive one another, what effect does it have on all the members?

3. **Explain how the teaching of Archbishop Vincent Nichols on the Power of Forgiveness could influence the moral values and behaviour of students in your school.**

4. **Why do you think a paper on the Power of Forgiveness has been included in the Mission of the Church?**

8.6 The Church in Britain

Religious Education Curriculum Directory
"The Church is at the same time a spiritual community and an historical, visible organisation. The Church is catholic, that is universal (of every time and place). Everyone is called to its catholic unity of the People of God: to it belong or are ordered the Catholic faithful, others who believe in Christ and finally all human people called by God's grace to salvation." (p. 19).

Attainment Target 1: Learning *about* the Catholic faith.
Attainment Target 2: Learning *from* the Catholic faith.

Key Learning Objectives:
- Know about the first arrival of the Gospel in Britain.
  o Reflect on the courage of the early Christians.

- Know about the first missionaries to Britain.
  o Reflect on the message they have for us today.

- Know about the Monastic Life in the Middle Ages in Britain. (DVD ROM)
  o Reflect on the importance of the monks and nuns for teaching the Gospel.

- Understand that there was a struggle between the Catholic Church and the State.
  o Reflect on the importance of making decisions about our Faith.

- Know how present day divisions among Christians arose.
  o Reflect on the importance of an informed conscience.

- Know about the dissolution of the Monasteries. (DVD ROM)
  o Reflect on the effect this had on society.

- Know about the Reformation in England and Wales.
  o Reflect on the consequences of it for us today.

- Know what is special about the Catholic Church.
  o Reflect on its links with other Christian denominations. (DVD ROM)

Theological Notes

Why is the Church Catholic or universal?
God revealed his purpose for all, in and through our Lord Jesus Christ. Our Lord died for everyone. He established his Church to hand on the revelation of that purpose to all nations and to bring to all, the invitation to accept the salvation won for them on Calvary. The Church is therefore universal in its mission.

What does 'catholic' mean?

"The word 'catholic' means 'universal', in the sense of 'according to the totality' or 'in keeping with the whole'. The Church is catholic in a double sense:

First, the Church is catholic because Christ is present in her. 'Where there is Christ Jesus, there is the Catholic Church.' In her subsists the fullness of Christ's body united with its head; this implies that she receives from him 'the fullness of the means of salvation' which he has willed: correct and complete confession of faith, full sacramental life, and ordained ministry in apostolic succession. The Church was, in this fundamental sense, catholic on the day of Pentecost and will always be so until the day of the Parousia.

Secondly, the Church is catholic because she has been sent out by Christ on a mission to the whole human race." CCC 830, 831

Why are there divisions among Christians?

Although the Church mediates God's call to eternal glory to all humankind, each person must personally respond to that call in order to be part of the catholic unity of the Church.

As the response of individuals and of nations has been varied, the catholic unity of the Church, which Christ established, does not extend to all who have heard the message proclaimed by the Church. Moreover, some cultures have been closed to the Word of God and have not been able to respond to it as yet. The work of making the message known to all peoples still goes on. Many men and women work in the mission-field to bring God's message to all. There are many religious orders dedicated to missionary work.

The one message of Christ, which he entrusted to his Church, has always been a subject of controversy. Just as our Lord met with disbelief, so do his messengers. Scandals, accidents of history, disagreements, intrigues, incomprehension etc. etc. have all affected the handing on of the message. This has resulted in divergence and mutual hostility. Many Christians differ, quite sincerely, on important doctrines. For instance, Luther struggled with problems of faith and broke away from the Catholic Church. Many today follow his lead. These differences have to be recognised. Equally, that people sincerely hold to these differences is a matter of fact. Up until recently, it was the differences that were emphasised. Today, emphasis is placed also on what Catholics have in common with other Christians. We recognise that all share the life of Christ through the working of the Holy Spirit.

Why are all people called to catholic unity?

All people are called to catholic unity because it is the will of God. Our Lord expressed this will when he prayed to his Father, "May they all be one. Father may they be one in us as you are in me and I am in you" (Jn. 17:21). Our Lord also said: "If you make my word your home you will indeed be my disciples, you will learn the truth and the truth will make you free" (Jn. 8:32). Unity results from all believing in the one truth of which Jesus is the full revelation and which he gave to his Church.

Many Christian Churches are now actively seeking the unity for which Christ prayed. They have entered into dialogue with one another. For Catholics, dialogue presumes that they are clear about what the Church teaches. The Church teaches, for instance, that: "It was to the apostolic college alone, of which Peter is the head, that we believe our Lord entrusted all the blessings of the New Covenant, in order to establish on earth the one Body of Christ in which all should be fully incorporated who belong in any way to the people of God" (Second Vatican Council - Decree on Ecumenism, No.3). "This Church, constituted and organised as a society in the present world, subsists in the Catholic Church, which is governed by the successor of St Peter and by the bishops in communion with him. Nevertheless many elements of sanctification and truth are found outside its visible confines. Since these are gifts belonging to the Church of Christ, they are forces impelling towards Catholic unity." (Decree on The Church, No.8).

The Decree on Religious Freedom recognises that faith is a free response to God's revelation. It does not encourage belief in the freedom to choose whatever religion we like. It teaches the obligation to seek the truth in all sincerity. Being brought up in other Christian religious traditions results in people sincerely holding positions at variance the Church's teaching. However, all who seek God with a sincere heart are on the way to salvation.

How does the Church today respond to divisions?

Christian missionaries found that their work was spoilt by the rivalry of the different denominations. At a meeting of 159 missionary societies in 1910, in Edinburgh, it was agreed that the historically rooted denominational divisions of Europe and N. America were generally irrelevant to the missionary task. This was the start of the ecumenical movement in its modern form.

However, the unity for which Christ prayed is a gift of the Spirit. Sincere prayer is essential, together with a willingness to respond to the prompting of the Spirit. There are many obstacles in the way of that unity and all need to co-operate according to their ability.

The Roman Catholic Church, conscious of possessing the essential unity which was Christ's gift to his Church, was slow to become involved in the ecumenical movement. However, the movement, under the impulse of God's Spirit, gathered momentum and the Church hammered out ways in which it could take part in this great movement of convergence.

For the Church, the principle regulating relations with other Churches is that:
   a) Jesus Christ brought the full revelation of the truth to the world for its salvation.
   b) He established One, Holy, Catholic and Apostolic Church to proclaim, develop and safeguard that truth until he comes again at the last day.
   c) The fullness of the truth which Jesus brought resides in the Catholic Church.

In 1964, the Second Vatican Council published its Decree on Ecumenism, *'Unitatis Redintegratio'*, concerning the restoration of unity among all Christians.

It draws up guidelines for dialogue with:

- the Orthodox Churches;
- the Reformation Churches;
- other Christian bodies.
- While the Council teaches the unique position of the Catholic Church as the Church established by Christ, it supports the ecumenical movement.
- It talks of **restoring** Christian unity rather than a **return** of fallen-away Christians to Roman Catholicism.
- It admits that both sides were to blame at the time of the Reformation.
- It teaches that many of the elements that properly belong to the Church of Christ may also exist outside the visible boundaries of the Catholic Church and are found in other separated Christian Churches and communities.

In 1965, the Council made a declaration on the relation of the Church to non-Christian religions, *'Nostrae Aetate'*.

- Without ceasing to preach Christ as the Way, the Truth and the Life, the Church rejects nothing of what is true and holy in these religions.
- It encourages dialogue in the search for spiritual and moral values.
- It states that special respect and understanding should be given to the Jews; they are not to be blamed for the death of Jesus Christ. It teaches that all kinds of persecution and discrimination are condemned.

In 1968, the Secretariat for Unbelievers, set up by the Council, published a document to guide Christians '**On Dialogue with Unbelievers**'.

In 1995, John Paul II published his Encyclical **'Ut Unum Sint'** (That all May be One), on commitment to Ecumenism. (The following numbers refer to paragraphs in CTS publication of UUS.)

"The commitment to ecumenism must be based upon conversion of hearts and upon prayer, which will also lead to the necessary purification of past memories." (2)

"The Catholic Church embraces with hope the commitment to ecumenism as a duty of the Christian conscience enlightened by faith and guided by love." (8)

"To believe in Christ means to desire unity." (9)

"Ecumenism is directed precisely to making the partial communion existing between Christians grow towards full communion in truth and charity." (14)

"The unity willed by God can be attained only by the adherence of all to the content of revealed truth in its entirety." (18)

"Love is the great undercurrent which gives life and adds vigour to the movement towards unity."

"When Christians pray together, the goal of unity seems closer." (22)

"One of the advantages of ecumenism is that it helps Christian communities to discover the unfathomable riches of the truth." (38)

"Unity of action leads to the full unity of faith." (40)

"The 'universal brotherhood' of Christians has become a firm ecumenical conviction." (42)

"With increasing frequency, Christians are working together to defend human dignity, to promote peace, to apply the Gospel to social life, to bring the Christian spirit to the world of science and of the arts." (74)

"The obligation to respect the truth is absolute. Is this not the law of the Gospel?" (79)

"Full unity will come about when all share in the fullness of the means of salvation entrusted by Christ to his Church." (86)

In 2000, the Congregation for the Doctrine of the Faith published *"Dominus Iesus"* on the unicity and salvific universality of Jesus Christ and the Church.

These are some of the ways in which the Church is responding to divisions.

On what is the catholic unity of the People of God based?

Our Lord gave authority to his Church to teach and to preserve the truth which his heavenly Father sent him into the world to reveal, by his life, death and resurrection. Through the working of the Holy Spirit, that truth is handed down from age to age. The handing on is called tradition from the Latin word 'traditio' which means 'handing down' or 'handing on'. The Holy Scriptures, formed under the inspiration of the Holy Spirit, express the revelation. The Church, by the working of the same Holy Spirit, is their authentic interpreter. The authority of the Church guards the revealed truth contained in the scriptures and handed down in the tradition.

Thus unity stems from all in the Church believing in the one truth as revealed by God. **Revealed truth** is the basis of this unity. It comes about by the gift of the Holy Spirit. The belief includes loyalty to the tradition and acceptance of the authority given to the Church by our Lord. Revealed truth is something given. It is not a matter of opinion. It is given so that we may believe. God guarantees its truth.

"The Christian economy, therefore, since it is the new and definitive Covenant, will never pass away; and no new public revelation is to be expected before the glorious manifestation of our Lord Jesus Christ. Yet even if Revelation is already complete, it has not been made completely explicit; it remains for Christian faith gradually to grasp its full significance over the course of the centuries." CCC 66

The necessary characteristics of a member of the Church are: belief that God has revealed the Way, the Truth and the Life necessary for our salvation; and fidelity to that truth handed down in the Sacred Scriptures under the authority given to his Church by Our Lord. By these, the Church manifests its unity to the world.

Additional Notes

The Reformation

"When Henry VIII succeeded to the throne in 1509, England was a Catholic country which looked to the pope as its spiritual head. Ten years later, when the first stirrings of Protestanism were felt across continental Europe, England remained loyal both to the pope and to the idea of a united Christendom. Indeed, in 1521, the conservative Henry denounced the teachings of the reformer Martin Luther and was rewarded with the title *Defender of the Faith*, still borne by British monarchs to this day.

Moving forward another ten years, however, a very different picture emerges. Henry was now in opposition to Pope Clement VII who had refused to grant the king's wish to divorce his first wife, Catherine of Aragon, and wed his mistress, Anne Boleyn. The dispute triggered a chain of events that revolutionised the religious landscape of England. Through a series of parliamentary acts, England 'broke' with Rome and the king became the supreme head of the Church of England. From this position, Henry oversaw a decade of reforms. Between 1535 and 1540, the monasteries of England and Wales were completely dissolved. In 1536, pilgrimages were abolished and in 1538 royal injunctions were issued against the burning of candles before images. By Henry's death in 1547, practices that had once been at the heart of medieval popular religion, such as the cult of saints, had been redefined as superstitious and idolatrous.

Why did the king's marital problem lead to a reformation in religious beliefs and practices?

This is a question that has fascinated historians for many years. It was once thought that the transformations initiated by Henry's government were timely interventions to cleanse a corrupt and moribund Church which had lost its way the end of the Middle Ages. However, the evidence available today suggests a very different scenario: that the people of England and Wales, on the very eve of the Reformation, were deeply satisfied with their traditional forms of faith. There appears no waning in the enthusiasm for traditional practices such as the cult of saints or attending Mass.

"It would be wrong to see England as a Protestant country under Henry VIII. The king took his role as head of the Church seriously and he would not tolerate radicals, denying many doctrines central to Protestanism, such as justification by faith alone. His curbs on freedom of expression meant that the path taken by the Reformation in England was complex, gradual and piecemeal. At the same time, the government had to take account of political threats from Catholic rulers abroad and from resistance at home...

On the whole, people did collaborate with the government in the sense that they dismantled shrines and informed against those who were loyal to the pope. Most noblemen, justices of the peace, clergy, churchwardens and constables obeyed the instructions given to them, not wishing to defy the power of the king. But it is difficult to know what people thought when they professed their loyalty, or why they wished to collaborate.

They would certainly have known that disobedience had serious consequences. Henry's response to Thomas More's opposition to the Act of Supremacy was a clear case in point: Thomas More was arrested, imprisoned in the Tower of London, and executed in July 1535... By the mid-sixteenth century, English people saw the relationship between Church and State very differently. They were now undertaking actions that they would never have dreamt of doing thirty or even twenty years before, such as plundering the monasteries and reading an English Bible. More changes were on the way. The destruction of Catholic practices took a step further under Henry's son, Edward VI: from 1547, iconoclasm was officially sanctioned and the foundation of Protestantism England was laid with the Book of Common Prayer (1549). Upheaval occurred again under Edward's sister, Mary, when, between 1553 and 1558, she set about reversing Protestant reforms and re-establishing Catholicism."

Abridged from 'The Reformation Period' by *Deborah Youngs*

The Recusant Period

"The Elizabethan settlement of 1559 brought to an end thirty years of religious change initiated by the Crown. During this period, England had lurched from Catholicism to Protestantism, back to Catholicism, and finally back to Protestanism. The settlement consisted of two acts of parliament: the Act of Supremacy which replaced the authority of the papacy in the English Church with that of the Crown; and the Act of Uniformity, which replaced the Latin, Catholic service books with the English, Protestant Book of Common Prayer. The clergy and the holders of public office were required to take an oath accepting the royal supremacy on pain of deprivation, and everyone was required to attend the new Sunday services of the Church of England on pain of a fine for each absence of one shilling (five new pence, but a good day's wage, in 1559). Such absence from church was the crime of *recusancy* (from the Latin verb, *recusare – to refuse)* and the guilty were called recusants."

Taken from 'The Recusant Period' by J.A. Hilton

> ## Know about the arrival of the Gospel in Britain.
> ## Reflect on the courage of the early Christians.

Starting Point:

This is an opportunity to help students recall the history of the very early Church as covered in 'The Way' for Year 7.

There is a choice of two activities:

WS 1: Make a collage of the **'Disciples journey of Faith'** in Students's Book page 108 with guidance in this book on page 103. It is also on the DVD ROM WS 1.

WS 2: Imagine you are a disciple.

Work in pairs: Imagine you are about twenty-five years old. You believe God is calling you to be a disciple to spread the Good News. Some young, enthusiastic people want to join you. Your first task is to prepare them by sharing what it was like for the first disciples.

These are only introductory activities so should take no more than one lesson.

Audio Recording: St. Alban.

Student's Book: Activity 2 on page 110. This is an opportunity for the teacher to help students
recap on some of the most important aspects of our Christian faith. See flipchart for answers.
If you do not have the DVD ROM answers to the questions can be found in the relevant sections of 'The Way'.

Flipchart: Alban and the Priest – answers to questions.

Assessment Folder: Assessment task on St. Alban.

> ## Know about the first missionaries to Britain.
> ## Reflect on the message they have for us today.

Starting Point:

Students will have covered the conversion of the Emperor Constantine in 'The Way' page 80.

In 312 AD, while preparing his army for battle, Constantine had a vivid dream. He saw a cross in the sky and on it were the words, 'In this sign you will conquer'. He understood that he was to put this sign on his soldiers' shields. Constantine won the battle and believed that the Christians' God had helped him. From that time on persecution of Christians by the Romans stopped.

 WS 3: St. Patrick.

 WS 4: St. Columba.

Other Resources Folder:
St. David
St. Aidan
St. Hilda

 PPP: St. David.

St. Augustine and the Benedictine Monks

 PPP: 'Angels not Angles' as an introduction to page 112 in the Students's Book.

 Assessment Folder: Assessment task on Alban.

> **Know about Monastic Life in the Middle Ages in Britain.**
> **Reflect on the importance of the monks and nuns for teaching the Gospel**

Note: This section is only on the DVD ROM.

 WS 5: Text and activities on **'Monastic life in the Middle Ages'.**

> **Understand that there was a struggle between the Church and State.**
> **Reflect on the importance of making decisions about our Faith.**

Background Notes: *Thomas was ordained a priest on 2nd June 1162 by Bishop Walter of Rochester. On the following day, Trinity Sunday, he was consecrated Archbishop of Canterbury. On Sunday 10th August, he assumed the pallium which had been sent by Pope Alexander III. It is said that Thomas took it from the High Altar of his cathedral himself. From the time of being ordained, Thomas' manner was said to have changed; he ate less and drank only water. To overcome the monks' opposition to a secular archbishop he went back to his old school at Merton and received the habit of a canon regular of St Augustine. Cf. 'St Thomas Becket' by Michael Green.*

Additional activities

1. Conflict between Church and State finally led to the death of Thomas Becket. Some people think it was a mistake for Thomas to have disagreed with the King. Discuss.
   - Say what you **think** and **why**;
   - give a different point of view and say why some people hold it;
   - say why you **disagree** with it;
   - try to give examples to support your opinion.

2. Work in small groups.
   a) Create one tableau (still scene) from the account of St. Thomas Becket and photograph it.
   b) Put your photo onto a sheet and annotate it making sure you have included and explained all the key information about your scene.
   (Further guidance and tips in Other Resources Folder on the DVD ROM.)

Research: Find out which famous authors have written about Thomas Becket or about Canterbury as a place of pilgrimage.

 Assessment Folder: Two Assessment tasks.

> **Know how divisions among Christians arose.**
> **Reflect on the importance of an informed conscience.**

Notes on Reformation, page 95.

Starting Point:

Students may have studied the Reformation in History. It is important to find out what they already know as this period has probably been taught from the Protestant view point and we are now looking at how it affected Catholics.

 PPP: Conscience: How do we form our conscience?
   - What is conscience?
   - How do we inform our conscience?
   - How do we know what our conscience is telling us is right?

Activities based on content of **PPP** on DVD ROM.

1. Imagine you are King Henry VIII. You are looking to divorce Catherine of Aragon in order to marry Anne Boleyn.
   a) Look back through each of the slides. Write down your inner thoughts to the questions on each slide.
   b) Did King Henry VIII make an informed decision? Give reasons.

2. Imagine you are Thomas More. You are asked to take the Oath of Supremacy to declare King Henry VIII Supreme Head of the Church in England.
   a) Look back through each of the slides. Write down your thoughts in response to the questions.
   b) Did Thomas More make an informed decision? Give reasons.

 Audio Recording: Extract from 'A Man for All Seasons' (Act II)
Listen to the recording of the Trial.

Other Resources: Script to dramatise Trial of Thomas More.

Additional Activities:
3. Thomas More wrote a famous book 'Utopia' which in Greek means 'No where, no place'. In it he described a perfect society.
   a) Describe your idea of 'Utopia', a perfect society.
   b) Explain what beliefs and values have inspired and influenced your idea.

4. a) Why do you think Pope John Paul II declared St. Thomas More 'Patron Saint' of politicians and statesmen?
   b) Give examples of what politicians could learn from him today.
      Think about:
      • family;
      • personal safety;
      • conscience;
      • public witness.

 Assessment Folder: Four assessment tasks.

Background information: Illustration of St. Thomas More, page 116 Student's Book, the writing on the scroll is 'I thank the Lord the field is won'; the bag in his hand shows he was chancellor. "Thomas More had an intuition of what was in store for him when he was summoned to appear before the Council at Lambeth on 13 April, 1534. He left his home and family at Chelsea with a heavy heart. As he was being rowed along the Thames, with his son-in-law William Roper, for a while he continued to be sad. Then he turned suddenly to Roper and said, with all his old confidence returned, **'Son Roper, I thank our Lord the field is won'**. He had already taken a decision which was to reach its final consequences on Tower Hill fifteen months later."
The King's good servant, but God's first by Thomas J. McGovern.

> ## Know about the dissolution of the Monasteries.
> ## Reflect on the effect this had on society.

Note: This section is only on the DVD ROM.

 WS 6: Dissolution of the Monasteries – text and activities.

> ## Know about the Reformation in England and Wales.
> ## Reflect on the consequences of it for us today.

Starting Point:

Explain that this is a period of rapid change in the history of England and Wales. It is only possible to give an overview of events with the focus on the impact it had on the Church.

Kings & Queens	Henry VIII 1509-1547 (Catholic)	Edward VI 1547-1553 (Protestant)	Mary I 1553-1558 (Catholic)	Elizabeth I 1558-1603 (Protestant)

 PPP: Priests' Hiding Holes.

 PPP: Some Martyrs of England & Wales.

 Audio Recording: St. Margaret Clitherow – an imaginary letter to a friend from prison.

Other Resources: copy of the letter from St Margaret Clitherow.

 Assessment Folder: Four assessment tasks.

Starting Point:

This is an opportunity to help students reflect on the freedom to worship which Catholics have today. When it was permitted to build churches many chose to build schools first. Discuss the reasons for this. *(For example, it was important to educate Catholics in the faith so that they would understand what they believe and why.)*

Activity

Freedom at last! What next?

    a) In groups, design an ACTION PLAN to meet the needs of the newly liberated community. Keep in mind the variety of needs:

- teach the faith;
- to worship together;
- organisation;
- money;
- meet the needs of the poor *(research the Religious Orders that came in from other Countries, e.g. Ireland and France)*.

    b) Decide as a group which of these is your priority. Justify your choice to the rest of the class.

**Know what is special about the Catholic Church.
Reflect on its links with other Christian denominations.**

Note: This section is only on the DVD ROM.

 WS 7: What is special about the Catholic Church?

 Audio Recording: Some changes in the Catholic Church after the Second Vatican Council.

Other Resources: Time-line.

Prayer

Lord God,
Help us to appreciate the gifts you offer us.
Send your Spirit to make us strong in faith
and active in good works. Amen

Journey of Faith of the Disciples

Resources:
'The Way' Students' Books and Power Point presentations for the:
- DVD ROM
- Bibles
- Access to Internet for pictures

To be completed within one lesson.

Work in small Groups.
Make a collage of the 'Journey of Faith of the Disciples'.

Group 1   Disciples witnessed the miracles Jesus worked:
           The Way, pages 46, 47, 48 and others.

Group 2   Disciples heard Jesus preach and teach:
           The Way, pages 43, 45, 50, 51, 52, 55.

Group 3   Jesus bids farewell; Pentecost:
           The Way, pages 62, 63, 64, 65.

Group 4   Stephen martyred, Saul's experience:
           The Way, pages 67, 68, 69.

Group 5   Blessings and challenges for disciples:
           The Way, pages 66, 70, 71.

Group 6   Persecution:
           The Way, pages 77, 78, 79, 80; The Way, PPP Catacombs.

Group 7   Paul shares his faith in God:
           The Way, pages 104 and 105.

Group 8   Death of the apostles:
           The Way, PPPs: Death of the Apostles, Paul's Martyrdom.

Acknowledgements

Grateful thanks to Deborah Youngs for permission to use an extract from her essay 'The Reformation Period' and to J.A. Hilton for permission to us an extract from 'The Recusant Period'. These essays are published in 'Held in Trust' 2008 years of Sacred Culture, St. Omer Press.

Permission credits

Cover photo: stained glass window © CWS Design, 9 Ferguson Drive, Lisburn BT28 2EX; forest © Anthia Cumming Dreamstime.com; Pen and Pad – used throughout © Kjpargeter Dreamstime.com; Wise Owl – used throughout © Joingate, Dreamstime.com; Peace Dove – used throughout © Ginesvaler Dreamstime.com; headphones, used throughout © Petrosq, Dreamstime.com; flipchart man, used throughout Dreamstime.com; LCD monitor, used throughout, © Scorpion26, Dreamstime.com; page 21 © Ryan's Well Foundation; pages 68, 69 and 71 © ITV Global Entertainment; page 70 © Jean-François Kieffer, One Thousand Gospel Images, Les Presses d'Ile de France; page 89 courtesy of the Marquette University Archives WI.

From the editor

How would you rate your prayer life?

Most Christians would answer: "Oh, not nearly as good as it should be". But that raises the potentially disturbing question: "Well, how good should it be?"

Should prayer flow out naturally from us, like fragrance from a flower? Should we be leaping out of bed in the morning, and positively sprinting to our chosen place for prayer, eager not to waste a second?

Well, one day we will speak to God like that (it's called 'heaven'), but in the meantime prayer will be a battle. We are still weighed down by sin and weakness, and like the disciples we find ourselves falling asleep on the job. We should expect, in other words, to struggle in prayer.

This is why the Bible is so full of exhortations to keep praying, and not to give up. "Continue steadfastly in prayer", Paul urges the Colossians, "being watchful in it with thanksgiving".

So perhaps a better question would be: *How is your prayer battle going?* Are you continuing to fight? Or have you laid down your weapons and surrendered? This is what many Christians mean when they say their prayer life is "not nearly as good as it should be". They have largely given up praying because it is too hard, and they are too busy, and life is pressing in, and things seem to go on by themselves anyway, and ... you know the rest of the excuses by heart.

The three articles in this MiniZine are designed to get you back on track. The first looks more closely at the reasons we don't pray; the second gives us a refresher in the basics of prayer to help us get started (or re-started); and the third discusses how our small groups can be a very significant encouragement and help to prayer.

I pray that the result will not just be guilt, but a rejuvenated enthusiasm to rejoin the battle of prayer.

TONY PAYNE

The articles in this MiniZine were first published in *The Briefing*, Matthias Media's monthly magazine. For more info, articles and subscription details go to **www.thebriefing.com.au**.

CONTENTS

© Matthias Media 2009

Matthias Media
(St Matthias Press Ltd ACN 067 558 365)
PO Box 225
Kingsford NSW 2032
Australia
Phone: (02) 9663 1478
International phone: +61-2-9663-1478
Email: info@matthiasmedia.com.au
Internet: www.matthiasmedia.com.au

Scripture quotations are from The Holy Bible, English Standard Version, copyright © 2001 by Crossway Bibles, a publishing ministry of Good News Publishers. Used by permission. All rights reserved.

ISBN 978 1 921441 51 6

Editor Tony Payne
Art & Design Joy Lankshear

Diagnosing a sick prayer life

AUTHOR 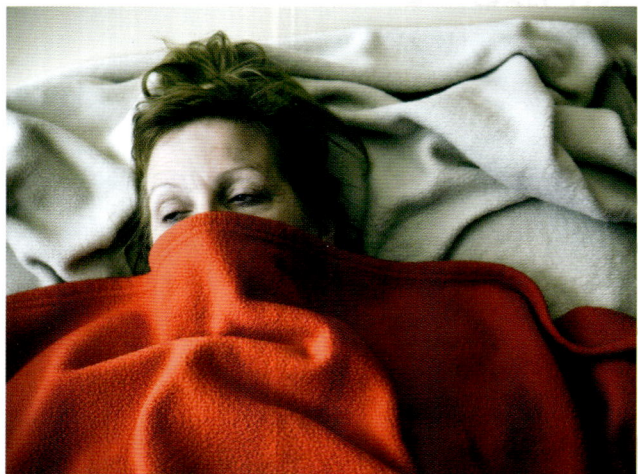 **TONY PAYNE**

Do you ever wonder whether you really are a Christian? In those moments when you can't go to sleep at night, and your mind has time to roam over the events of the day and the week, do you ever find yourself thinking, "Am I just kidding myself that all this is true and that it's really changed my life?

Am I really any different from how I was last year or the year before that? If God's Spirit is in me, why does my old nature keep showing its ugly head? If other people knew what I was really like, they'd be horrified. I feel like such a phoney sometimes."

In my experience, both personally and in talking with friends, nothing evokes these sorts of feelings more strongly than our struggles with prayer. We know prayer is good, and a privilege, and a blessing. We know that the Bible calls us and commands us to pray. There is every reason to pray—

but we don't. Or if we do, it tends to be short, perfunctory, irregular.

"Why?!" we find ourselves asking in the middle of the night. "I love the Lord. I love being a Christian. I have no desire to be anything else. So why do I find prayer such a struggle? Why is my Christian life blooming in knowledge and in ministry to others, but quietly dying in prayer?"

A DIAGNOSIS

At one level, a diagnosis for our problems in prayer is very easy to arrive at, if rather depressing: we are sinful, stubborn fools. That's why we fail to pray. In fact, that's why we fail to love people, tell the truth, be patient, and a thousand other patently good things that we want to do but fail to do.

Sin is a chronic disease that will never be cured this side of glory. And although the constant presence of God's Spirit in our lives alleviates the symptoms, and may even improve our quality of life (as it were), the disease will always be with us. The treatment is a lifetime of repentance and faith. And because of the death and resurrection of Christ, the outcome is not terminal.

All the same, as true as this simple diagnosis is, we need to probe a little deeper. We need to ask: What form does our sinful, stubborn foolishness take with respect to prayer? What kind of spiritual malady overtakes us such that we fail to pray? Armed with a more detailed diagnosis, we might be in a position to apply the treatment more effectively.

In the remainder of this article, we'll look at *three spiritual viruses* that infect our brains and lay low our prayer lives. We catch

4

these viruses from the world around us, from our friends, from our upbringing, and from false teaching we might have received. Regardless of how we pick them up, these viruses distort our view of God and prayer, and make our prayer lives sick.

No doubt these are not the only three, but they are very common and they infect the heart of prayer—that is, our understanding of who God is, and how we relate to him.

VIRUS 1: WE DOUBT THAT GOD IS ABLE

Christian prayer is based on who God is. We can only go to God and ask him for things if he is the kind of God who is willing to accept us into his presence and to listen to us. And there would be no point approaching this God and making requests of him if he wasn't able to do something in response to our requests.

This seems obvious enough, and indeed it is written all over the Bible. God is supremely powerful and able. Jeremiah begins a famous prayer by exclaiming: "Ah, Lord GOD! It is you who have made the heavens and the earth by your great power and by your outstretched arm! Nothing is too hard for you" (Jer 32:17).

This refrain—'nothing is impossible for God'—runs throughout the Scriptures. It reflects the Bible's view that everything is under God's control: he created all things; he sustains all things by his powerful word. He's the supreme lord of everything.

However, surely if we believed this, we would go to this all-powerful God at every possible opportunity to ask him to intervene in the events of our world—to do things, to change things, to act.

Our lack of prayer suggests that perhaps we don't really believe God is so powerful after all. We're infected with an unbelief in the power of God to work in our lives. This unbelief comes in two forms.

Type A: Misunderstanding nature and super-nature

As modern people, we have been taught to divide everything that happens into two categories: natural and supernatural. There are the natural, ordinary, scientifically provable things that happen; and then there are the inexplicable, weird, 'supernatural' things that you just shrug your shoulders about.

This is not a biblical way of thinking at all. God can use natural means to achieve natural results, such as simply sending the rain to water the earth and produce crops. But he can also use natural means to achieve extraordinary results—such as sending a strong east wind to drive back the Red Sea and allow the Israelites to cross on dry land (Exod 14:21). Or God can suspend the normal, natural pattern of his creation by making a man dead for four days come back to life (John 11 38-44). All of these are equally the work of the powerful, sovereign God of all the world.

If we are infected with the modern view —and all of us have been taught it explicitly and implicitly since we were kids—God gets parked off into the world of weird phenomena and unexplained events. He becomes a last resort when all 'natural' means have failed; or perhaps a supplier of psychological strength and calm to deal with the ups and downs of daily life.

Christians who are infected with this way of thinking about God and the world can end up virtually prayerless. If, deep down, we don't think that God is actually able to act or intervene to change anything in the course of our daily lives, but is only going to give us a bit of fortitude to put up with things as they are, then prayer doesn't seem so urgent or necessary. We can just get on with managing things ourselves, firing off the occasional brief request for some extra patience and perseverance.

This is a grave danger for modern Christians, especially those living in the prosperous West. We live in a technological society, where most diseases seem easily curable and where life is, for the most part, secure, comfortable and healthy. If we don't take active steps to the contrary, our default way of thinking about the world will be that life goes on very normally without God—that

> Our lack of prayer suggests that perhaps we don't really believe God is so powerful after all. We're infected with an unbelief in the power of God to work in our lives.

5

he doesn't really do anything in the world any more, and that his activity is limited to making us feel a bit better. At most, we might be driven to prayer in desperation when things fall apart. But our implicit, daily belief—reinforced by the media, the education system and our interaction with others—is that God is impotent to intervene and actually do anything of any significance in our world. He may have set the world going, but he doesn't bother with it much these days.

If we are wondering why our prayer lives might be ailing, perhaps it is because we are infected with this unbiblical way of thinking. Perhaps we have ceased to believe that God is supremely able to work in his world, through both normal everyday means and extraordinary inexplicable means. Perhaps we have developed a subtle scepticism about the limits of his power.

Type B: Misunderstanding God's sovereign will

The second form of our doubt that God is really able to act and intervene in response to our prayers has to do with God's unchangeable sovereign will. This view states that if God is completely in control and has his plans for the world and for each one of us, then whatever else prayer might achieve, it cannot alter God's plans. God will do what God will do, whether we pray or not. Prayer may have beneficial effects on *us* (in increasing our daily trust in him, for example), but it has no effect on God himself. Otherwise, how can God be sovereign?

> **The Bible certainly affirms the absolute sovereignty and power of God over his creation at every moment, and his determination to work his plans and purposes out. But it never takes that to mean that God is deaf to our prayers.**

In this view, God remains supremely powerful, but his hands are completely tied (as it were) by his preordained plans. There's no point asking him for anything because he is not able to change his plans to grant us our request—unless he was going to give it to us anyway, in which case he would have done so whether we prayed or not. So what's the point of praying?!

Again, this is a distortion of the Bible's view of God's sovereignty. It has to be a distortion because the Bible contradicts this view on so many occasions!

What does "You do not have, because you do not ask" mean in James 4:2 if God does not respond to our prayers by giving us things? Or what are we to make of the many instances in the Old Testament which speak of God 'relenting' in response to heartfelt prayers, and not visiting upon people the wrath and destruction he had intended (e.g. Exod 32:9-14; Jer 26:19; Joel 2:13)? Why would God promise us that we could "call upon me in the day of trouble; I will deliver you" (Ps 50:15) if our calling upon him had no effect—that is, if the outcome of the day of trouble would have been precisely the same, according to God's eternal will, whether we had prayed or not? And what do these words about Elijah mean if not that God acts in response to human prayers?

> The prayer of a righteous person has great power as it is working. Elijah was a man with a nature like ours, and he prayed fervently that it might not rain, and for three years and six months it did not rain on the earth. Then he prayed again, and heaven gave rain, and the earth bore its fruit. (Jas 5:16b-18)

The Bible certainly affirms the absolute sovereignty and power of God over his creation at every moment, and his determination to work his plans and purposes out. But it never takes that to mean that God is deaf to our prayers—that they rebound without effect from the hard, shiny surface of his eternal decrees. Quite the contrary; Scripture everywhere assumes that God will graciously *respond* to his people's prayers and *include their prayers* in his sovereign plans. Just as God works in and through the 'natural' events of our world in his sovereign way, so he works in and through our prayers to achieve his purposes. When we stop believing that God really listens to and responds to our prayers, we stop praying.

VIRUS 2: WE DOUBT THAT GOD IS WILLING

Even if the effectiveness of prayer is granted and God's ability to act is accepted, there is still the problem of his willingness to act. For the Christian, this at first seems like a blasphemous suggestion. God not willing to act for our benefit? How absurd!

However, we feel this virus creeping up on us in the face of suffering. Why did God not intervene to stop the Asian tsunami? Why does my life continue to be dogged with illness and heartache? Why did he let my child become so sick?

The Bible's answer—very briefly—is that God very often achieves his purposes and answers our prayers *through hard times, not by delivering us from them*. Sin and evil do not thwart his plans. On the contrary, he is able to work through the evil that we do in order to achieve his good purposes. We see this again and again in the Bible, such as when Joseph says to his lying, treacherous brothers, "... you meant evil against me, but God meant it for good ..." (Gen 50:20). We see it even more classically in the cross of Jesus, where the most incredible evil and suffering took place— and yet God was behind it all, achieving the most extraordinary victory (Acts 2:22-24).

When times are tough, or when God's answer to our prayer is not what we had hoped for—when we pray like Paul three times for the thorn in the flesh to be taken away, and it remains—it's then that we start to doubt whether God really has our good in mind. We begin to question his generosity or goodness.

The antidote to this spiritual virus is to inject our minds with the clear promises of our heavenly Father: that he cares for us (1 Pet 5:6-7), that he longs to give us every good gift (Matt 7:11) and that even the smallest and most insignificant matter is not beneath his attention (Matt 10:29-31).

> **Why did God not intervene to stop the Asian tsunami? Why does my life continue to be dogged with illness and heartache?**

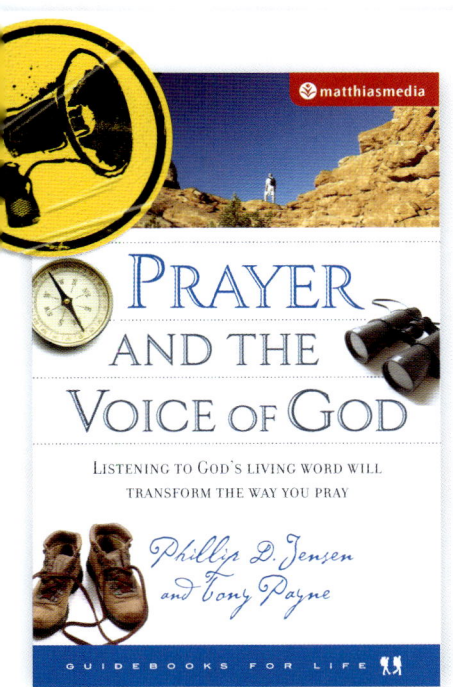

Prayer doesn't have to be a mystery or a burden. In *Prayer and the Voice of God*, Phillip Jensen and Tony Payne open up what God himself says to us in the Scriptures about prayer, including what prayer really is, why we should do it and why we often don't.

This insightful, practical book offers powerful motivations to get us back on our knees and praying, as well as helpful discussions of what to pray for.

A clear, readable guide for new Christians wanting to get started in prayer, or longer-serving Christians whose prayer lives are wilting.

This is a good little book and one that I think would prove very useful for personal reading or for group study, for the format and study guide would lend themselves well to discussion in a group setting. I am pleased to recommend it for either purpose and trust others will benefit from it as I have. (www.challies.com review)

Prayer and the Voice of God is part of Matthias Media's Guidebooks for Life series: easy-to-read, practical Christian books dealing with key Christian topics from a biblical perspective.

For more information about other Matthias Media resources please visit our website or call us for a free resource guide.

matthiasmedia
two ways to live. one life to give.

AUSTRALIA **1800 814 360** (SYDNEY **9663 1478**) | **www.matthiasmedia.com.au**
UNITED STATES **1-866-407-4530** | **www.matthiasmedia.com**

VIRUS 3: WE MISUNDERSTAND OUR RELATIONSHIP WITH GOD

The first two viruses attack our understanding of who God really is and what he is like—and thus make our prayer sick. This third one focuses more on our relationship with God.

Again, there are two varieties of this problem.

Type A: We underestimate our sin and the privilege of access

Firstly, we forget or underestimate just what an incredible privilege is our access to God in prayer. In our own minds, it's amazing how easily we magnify our goodness, and diminish the righteousness of God. We lose sight of how blindingly pure and good God is, and how profoundly sinful we are. It's possible, of course, that we never really understood this idea in the first place. We may have glided into Christianity without ever having squarely confronted the depths of our own lostness, or the heights of God's holiness. More commonly, however, we just drift away from this understanding.

> **If we give up the fight and simply acquiesce in sin as if it doesn't matter, then we are in grave spiritual danger, and should take immediate action.**

A mental virus weakens our very grasp on the gospel itself—that a sinful wretch like me could approach the holy God, and, rather than being excluded or destroyed by his holiness, be welcomed through the Lord Jesus and granted free access to his throne!

Our relationship with God through the gospel is the basis of prayer. It's a privilege beyond imagining. Yet over time it becomes a very small thing in our eyes.

As a parent, I sometimes splutter with outrage at the way my kids take all their privileges and comforts and advantages for granted. And yet I'm really no better. I take for granted the incredible relationship God has initiated with me, the glorious privilege of having access to the throne of grace. And so I no longer avail myself of it.

Type B: We think faith is a feeling

We also misunderstand our relationship with God if we think that feelings are its barometer. Our relationship with God is an objective fact, but our feelings vary widely from hour to hour in response to all kinds of stimuli.

'Faith' is not a mysterious religious feeling or quality; it is trust, reliance and dependence on God. And the important thing about trust is not how strong the trust is or what it feels like, but whether the thing you're trusting in is trustworthy.

Do you think you are less of a Christian when you feel sad or low or discouraged? Or do you think you are less of a Christian when you are sick or suffering or tired?

If you do, then perhaps what you are really trusting in or relying upon is not Christ himself but the quality of your 'faith'. This is a relatively common mistake. It's not our faith that gets us right with God and saves us; it is Christ who saves us through his atoning death and glorious resurrection. He has done the work. Our job is simply to trust in his incredible trustworthiness. How this feels will change from day to day. But Jesus Christ does not change—he is the same yesterday and today and forever (Heb 13:8).

The same is true of prayer, which is a verbal expression of our faith. Sometimes we will feel very much like praying. Sometimes we won't. Sometimes prayer feels sweet and delightful; at other times, it feels like a wrestling match; and at other times, we feel as if the heavens are silent and distant, and that our prayers are going nowhere.

These feelings are natural and common (to sinful people like us), but they are no indication of the quality of our prayers or the extent to which God has heard them. Indeed, if we wait until we feel like praying, some of us might never pray again.

If we make the mistake of thinking that we need to be in a certain mood, or feel a certain way, before prayer is really legitimate, we have caught a nasty version of Virus 3.

IS THERE LIFE IN THE PATIENT?

The sick state of our prayer lives can (and should) disturb us. Hopefully, having looked at some of the misunderstandings that contribute to the problem, we are in a better position to keep in step with the Spirit and vigorously pursue a healthier prayer life.

As we do so, we shouldn't despair. Failing to pray doesn't render us non-Christian, any more than failing to love does, or failing to rejoice, or failing to be generous, or failing in all the other areas in which we all fail. To paraphrase the words of John: "I have written all this so that you will pray, but if you don't pray, remember you have an advocate with the Father, Jesus Christ the righteous ...". Prayerlessness will be a lifelong struggle for us; we shouldn't think that the struggle is wrong, or indicative that we have ceased to be Christian.

We shouldn't despair, but neither should we give up. As in any other area of the Christian life, if we give up the fight and simply acquiesce in sin as if it doesn't matter, then we are in grave spiritual danger, and should take immediate action.

The difficult thing about the sin of prayerlessness is that it's a secret sin. No-one knows—except the One person who matters, of course.

If our prayer lives have sunk to the stage of being in a coma, we need to do something about it. If praying is just not something we do any more, then the Bible has an important word for us: Repent!

You may need to start small and grow. Think of a few spots in your week when you are regularly in the same place, or doing the same thing—some regular pattern of life to which you could tie a short time of personal prayer—and start there. Read a Bible passage to get you thinking about who God is, and how good he is to pray to, and then spend even just a few minutes bringing your requests before the heavenly Father.

Contrary to the insidious voices that we sometimes find in our heads, he is very able, very willing, and through Jesus very ready to listen to our requests, and to grant us every good thing. ✪

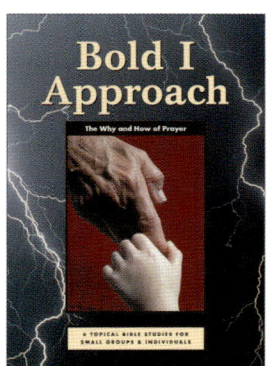

For many Christians, just the mention of the word 'prayer' is enough to arouse feelings of guilt, failure and confusion. However, when we turn to what God says about prayer in the Bible, we find that prayer is not nearly as complicated or difficult as we sometimes make it.

In six challenging and encouraging Bible studies, *Bold I Approach* looks at the glories and struggles of Christian prayer—what it is, why we do it, how we do it, and why we don't do it! Also included is an appendix of practical advice from Don Carson.

Whether you're a novice in prayer wondering where to start, or a veteran trying to get back on track, *Bold I Approach* will point you in the right direction.

Prayer is an almost universal human activity. Every day, around the world billions pray—to spirits, to Allah, to Buddha, to idols. But how are the prayers of the Christian different? Is there such a thing as 'Christian prayer'? In these five short talks, Phillip Jensen explains the biblical foundations of this most simple yet profound activity: To whom do we pray? Why pray? How to pray? What to pray for? What happens when we pray?

This is an ideal series for anyone—from the experienced Christian prayer warrior to the non-Christian curious to understand how they can pray.

The basics of prayer

AUTHOR  **PAUL GRIMMOND**

What is prayer? There are almost as many different ideas about prayer as there are people in the world. In some religions, prayer is a religious duty that keeps you in God's good books.

Other religions have prayer wheels or incense where participation in the activity itself (i.e. burning the incense or spinning the wheel) is considered a communication with God. In other places, prayer is silent meditation. But none of these ideas express what Jesus meant when he talked about prayer. For Jesus, prayer was simply *talking to God*.

In fact, prayer can be easily understood by looking at the two parts of this statement. Firstly, prayer is *talking*—expressing to God in words (either out loud or silently) what's in our heart. The kind of words isn't very important—Jesus condemned people who used fancy words when they prayed so that other people would think they were important. He also condemned people who used lots of words for the same reason. You don't need to pray for a long time to be heard; you just have to speak honestly to God.

One of the great promises that God makes in the death and resurrection of Jesus is that you are now his child. And as his child, you can bowl up and talk to him any time you like. You can pray when you walk or when you sit or when you kneel. You can even pray when you're driving the car if you want to (although not if you prefer to pray with your eyes closed!). Finally, because we're his children, God wants us to feel free to pray to him about anything we like— nothing is too big or small to bring to God.

But that brings me to the second part of the statement. Prayer is talking *to God*. While it's good to remember the incredible access we have to the God who made the whole universe, it's also good to remember who we're talking to when we talk to the God who made the universe. He is our creator and our saviour and our judge.

This will have certain implications. For example, instead of coming and telling God what *he* should do, we should come to him humbly to make our requests, recognizing that he knows better than we do. Sometimes God will answer our prayers in a totally different way than we expect (or want). In fact, God's answer to some of our requests may well be 'no'. We need to remember that God promises to work in everything for our good—to make us like Jesus. He will always answer our prayers according to what's best for us.

However, all of this probably leaves us with a question: *What should we pray about?* Probably the best way to answer the question is to investigate the prayer that Jesus taught his disciples to pray. It's sometimes called 'The Lord's Prayer', and it goes like this:

> Our Father in heaven,
> Hallowed be your name,
> Your kingdom come,
> Your will be done on earth as it is in heaven.
> Give us today our daily bread,
> And forgive us our sins as we forgive
>   those who sin against us.
> Lead us not into temptation but deliver us
>   from evil,
> For the kingdom, the power and the glory
>   are yours,
> Now and forever,
> Amen.[1]

Our Father in heaven

The first words of the prayer are a really important reminder of who we're praying to—our heavenly Father who has given up his Son to make us his children, the heavenly Father who is greater than any earthly father. If you've been hurt or abused by your father, then the word father may be a really painful one. Please know that God isn't like any human father. He loves us more deeply than we can ever know. Human fatherhood is supposed to mirror what God is like as a father. If your father wasn't like that, then he hasn't been what he was supposed to be. When Christians pray, we pray to our perfect Father who dwells in heaven as the Lord of all, and yet who loves us more than we can ever understand.

Hallowed be your name, Your kingdom come, Your will be done on earth as it is in heaven

The next part of the prayer tells us to pray in the light of who God is. As we know God better and understand what he wants for our world, we ask him to do his will in our world. The word 'hallowed' just means to 'make holy'. So the first line of the prayer asks God to work so that his name is seen as holy and precious in his world. This request goes hand in hand with the next couple of lines where we ask for God's will to be done on earth. God is treated as God and his name is made holy when people do what he wants them to do. What we're effectively praying is that God will make us more like Jesus and work in others to make them like Jesus too. That's the most important prayer that we can ever pray, for ourselves or anyone else.

Give us today our daily bread

In God's kindness, even as we pray for his will to be done, he also encourages us to pray for our needs—"give us today our daily bread". As the powerful, ruling king, God is in control of everything in his world. He gives every good gift and he is always able to answer our prayers. So we can pray to him about anything and everything. We can pray for food and for shelter, for help in relationships and for strength to do things we don't want to do.

But not only *can* we pray for these things, we *should* be praying for them. In a world of supermarkets and farming conglomerates, it's easy to think that milk comes from the bottle or from the factory. Ultimately, though, everything we eat comes from the generous hand of God. When we pray for these things, we are acknowledging that everything we have comes from God.

But the concrete nature of this prayer is also another reminder of God's tenderness and care. One of my favourite verses in the Bible says, "... do not be anxious about anything, but in everything by prayer and supplication with thanksgiving let your requests be made known to God" (Phil 4:6). There is nothing in our lives so big that God cannot deal with it, or so small that God does not care. He encourages us to come to him, because he's the only one who can meet our needs.

And forgive us our sins as we forgive those who sin against us

Jesus then reminds us to pray regularly for our greatest need—the forgiveness of our sins. I personally find this part of the Lord's Prayer very helpful, because it reminds me that I will always need forgiveness. Becoming a Christian means seeking to live God's way, but it doesn't mean instant perfection. It means ongoing forgiveness for our lack of perfection. It's so important to understand this, because after a while you can begin to wonder what's wrong with you—why do you keep sinning?

> **Instead of coming and telling God what *he* should do, we should come to him humbly to make our requests, recognizing that he knows better than we do.**

At this point, the Lord's Prayer presents one of God's great truths—even when you've been a Christian for thirty years, and even when you've sinned for the ten thousandth time, the only way to keep going in relationship with God is to come to him and ask for forgiveness. And each time we come, God forgives us in exactly the same way he forgave us at the very beginning. He listens to the intercession of his Son, who says to him, "I died and rose again for that one. I've borne the punishment for his sin. He trusts me and belongs to me. You can forgive him."

Lead us not into temptation but deliver us from evil

The next line of the prayer asks God to help us live for him. We don't want to be under the power of sin, and we don't want to follow where it leads, and so we ask God not to lead us into temptation but to deliver us from evil. Again, the reminder is that we can't do this by ourselves. By our own strength we will never be able to deal with evil; we need God to be at work in us to deliver us from evil.

For the kingdom, the power and the glory are yours, now and forever, Amen

The prayer finishes where it started, with a reminder that we ultimately seek the glory and honour of God—the mighty Lord who is establishing his kingdom. Jesus rules already, and one day the whole world will see him ruling when he returns in glory. The powerful one who holds the future of the world in his hands is our God, and we can pray to him with confidence knowing he wants to do what is best for us. How good is that!

> **The Lord's Prayer presents a model for us. It reminds us to pray about the things that are most important to God.**

IT'S NOT NECESSARY THAT WE REPEAT the exact words of the Lord's Prayer, as if they have special magical power. The Lord's Prayer presents a model for us. It reminds us to pray about the things that are most important to God (because we live in God's world), but it also encourages us to pray about *everything*, because God is our loving Father and he wants to hear from us.

When we see all of these truths printed on the page, prayer seems to be the most logical and sensible and wonderful thing in the world. But unfortunately, our sinful side easily gets the better of us—at least, that's what keeps happening to me. In spite of the privilege that we have in talking to God, many Christians find it easy to forget to pray. As with Bible reading, prayer needs to be built into the structure of our lives. For example, I try to remember to pray each day as I walk to and from work. By tying prayer to something that I do every day, it helps me to pray every day.

Another thing I've found helpful is to have a list of people and things to pray for, broken up into days. But I number the days rather than naming them. Each day I pray for the next day on the list, and if I miss one occasionally, I don't worry about it too much. On the list I have the names of my friends and family that I want to be praying for. I pray that God will help them to become more like Jesus, which for some of them means that I am praying for them to become a Christian for the first time. I also pray for some missionaries I know, and for people in my church. Sometimes there are specific things I need to be praying about—like when people are sick—but at other times I just pray for things that God tells me people need most. I pray that they will be living out the new life they have in Christ.

Many people I know tie their prayer and Bible reading together. So when they set aside twenty minutes a day to read the Bible, they then spend time in prayer in light of what they have read. This means that the things in the Bible become the things they pray for—whether for themselves or their friends and family. It's a really helpful pattern. With all of these things, it usually takes some time to experiment and find a method and a time of the day that works for you. And sometimes, you'll find a pattern works for a while and then stops working. When that happens, take the initiative and try something a bit different. But most importantly, keep reminding yourself why you read the Bible and pray. It's because you want to know and relate to the God who made you and who has given you new life. ✪

*This short article is adapted from Paul Grimmond's new book, **Right Side Up: Life as God meant it to be,** published by Matthias Media. See www.matthiasmedia.com for details.*

ENDNOTE

1.   This is the common form of the Lord's Prayer that is said by Christians and churches around the world. The actual text of the prayer can be found in the Bible in Matthew 6:9-13 and Luke 11:2-4.

Praying in small groups

AUTHOR 🕸 **COLIN MARSHALL**

Most Christian small groups pray. Most Christian groups easily drift into prayer ruts. Our times of prayer become hurried intercessions, a quick vote of thanks at the end of the Bible study, prayers for the sick or 'those who aren't with us', or general prayers for more love and wisdom. Of course, these are all great things to pray for, but we usually end up praying for them *by default*, because we don't put in the time and effort to think about what to pray.

Most groups find it easier to do Bible study (or have supper) than to pray. Prayer gets reduced to a minimum, sometimes included only to relieve our guilt about it.

This is not how we want it to be. We want our groups to *love* praying—to long to pray to God. We want to obey the Bible's urging to "continue steadfastly in prayer, being watchful in it with thanksgiving" (Col 4:2).

Our group meetings can be training grounds for great prayer warriors. How could your small group "continue steadfastly in prayer"? Here are eight pointers for better small group prayer.

1. Set an example
If you are a group leader, you must first address prayer in your own life. The group will see whether you are a prayer warrior or a prayer wimp. Enough said.

2. Give prayer priority in group time
You may need to be creative in order to achieve this. Occasionally, devote the entire meeting to prayer. Start your meeting with prayer instead of leaving it until the end. Pray at several different points during the meeting. Pray spontaneously as issues arise from discussion.

3. Keep track of the groups prayer concerns
Some groups use a 'Prayer Diary', so they can look back to what they have prayed about, as well as writing in specific events, people and occasions to pray for in the future. It is a very helpful aid to memory.

4. Be confident in God through Christ
Ultimately, this is what drives us to pray. It is the truth of the gospel—that we are lost on our own, but have entered into relationship with God through Christ—that will sustain us in prayer. We need to keep teaching the gospel. It reveals the love of the Father in his Son for his people. If we doubt that God cares for us and hears and responds to our prayers, we will never pray.

5. Move beyond 'collecting prayer points'
The old routine of collecting prayer points is a mixed blessing. It is good to hear people's concerns so that we can pray very specifically. It is one of the key ways we express our love for each other. But this routine does present some problems. It takes a lot of time, and the actual praying often gets tacked on the end of the discussion. It can become repetitive, with the same issues being raised every week. It can be difficult at certain stages of the group's existence for people to be honest and open with their prayer requests. The main problem, however, with sharing prayer points is that it promotes self-centred praying.

Our prayers are often of a totally different character to the prayers of the Bible. For example, look at the prayers in 2 Samuel 7:18-29 and Matthew 6:5-15 and Colossians 1:3-14. These prayers focus on the grand purposes of God; the salvation of Israel through David's dynasty; the growth of the gospel and of believers; the coming of the Kingdom of God; the renown of God. In short, they are God-centred, not self-centred, prayers. They are full of thanks to God, rehearsing his holiness and saving power, and asking him to fulfil his plans to save the world.

Paul sets an agenda for prayer meetings in 1 Timothy 2:1-7. We are to pray for everyone, with the focus upon godly living and the salvation of all. Of course, we can also bring our personal needs to God in prayer (see 1 Pet 5:7; Matt 6:25-34). By bringing all matters to God, even the minor details of our lives, we express faith in God's rule over all things. God has committed himself to provide and care for us.

Try different ways of collecting personal prayer points. For example, focus on some challenge to personal godliness that came up in the Bible study, and then ask each person to take a minute to reflect on how these bigger concerns of God connect with their own lives. Then pray specifically about these things. Or ask each person to share something that they have learnt recently from their own Bible reading, or from the sermons at church; and then pray about those things.

6. Be outward-looking

Following on from point 5, don't just pray for each other. Pray for the work of God more broadly:

- The group might adopt a missionary or evangelist for whom they can pray, as they keep track of his or her activities and needs.
- Pray for the salvation of your unbelieving friends and families. Pray more widely for the conversion of those in positions of power, of people who have a public profile, or even of neighbours whom you don't know.
- Pray for your church's programmes and plans. Perhaps adopt a particular ministry, such as Sunday School, and pray for it for a period.

7. Help group members learn to pray

It can be hard to get everyone in a group to pray out loud, especially when the group is quite new and people are not yet comfortable with each other. How can we make this easier for each other?

When we pray with others, we are not only praying to God, we are also leading others in prayer. This is true in any Christian context, such as conferences, committees and church. We must be conscious of others, not in order to impress them; on the contrary, we must seek to serve them. To help others learn to pray in your small group:

- Use the plural pronouns 'we' and 'our'. This signals that we are all praying, not just the person speaking.
- Say short prayers so that everyone can maintain attention.
- Avoid jargon or complicated expressions; use language that everyone in the group will understand.
- Don't switch into an unnatural 'prayer mode'. Use your normal voice and keep a normal posture.
- Form smaller groups. Reducing your group size into twos or threes for prayer can lower people's anxieties and allow them to pray more openly. Single sex prayer groups can have the same effect.

8. Form prayer partnerships

To foster prayer, some small groups form 'prayer partnerships', where two group members meet regularly to pray outside of the small group meeting. This not only deepens friendships, but gets the group members praying more, for each other and for broader concerns. There are many ways to set up prayer partnerships:

- Meet weekly or fortnightly outside the group to pray.
- Pray specifically for each other during the week, without meeting together.
- Break into prayer partners to share and pray during group time (this is especially useful early in the life of the group, when people are still getting to know each other).
- Change prayer partners every two to three months.

PRAYER IS ALWAYS A BATTLE, because the Christian life is a battle. Prayer doesn't always come easily or naturally. But in his kindness, God has given us each other to encourage each other to keep trusting him—and that includes encouraging each other to keep praying. Let's make good use of our small groups to urge, encourage, help and lead one another to continue steadfastly in prayer. ✪